MW00354355

SCULPTING
IN
WIRE

THE BASICS OF SCULPTURE

SCULPTING IN WIRE

Cathy Miles

A&C Black • London

CONTENTS

(Above) *A variety of butterflies from the butterfly project.* Photo by Simon Winnall.

(Pages 4–5) **The Party Politics Tea Set** *by Cathy Miles, 2005. Iron wire and assorted found material. Spot-welded.*

'**The Party Politics Tea Set** *came about through a little story I wrote about a political party conference. Attending, there was Prime Minster Goldfinch and Treasurer Tit, however, they could not keep an attentive audience as all the birds ploughed into tea and cake! This series of work got me interested in drawing objects with a perceived function. I enjoy what the piece gives you when the function has been removed.'*

Photo by Tas Kyprianou.

ACKNOWLEDGEMENTS

The development of creative skill and craftsmanship is a roller-coaster ride and a remarkable revolving personal journey. I would like to thank my immensely talented tutors, who were there at key pivotal points during my journey, in particular Simone ten Hompel for her unwavering support and guidance, for which I am sincerely grateful.

Thanks must also go to the makers who kindly contributed to this book, along with my partner Daniel for his invaluable help and who patiently and painstakingly photographed the practical processes. I must also thank my family for their love and practical support, without which I would be nowhere. Lastly, thank you to Alison Stace, who gave me the opportunity to write this book.

First published in Great Britain in 2009
A & C Black Publishers Limited
36 Soho Square
London W1D 3QY
www.acblack.com

Copyright © 2009 Cathy Miles

ISBN 978 0 7136 8887 0

CIP Catalogue records for this book are available from the British Library.

All rights reserved. No part of this publication may be reproduced in any form or by any means – graphic, electronic or mechanical, including photocopying, recording, taping or information storage and retrieval systems – without the written permission of A&C Black Publishers Limited.

Cathy Miles has asserted her right under the Copyright, Design and Patents Act 1988 to be identified as the author of this work.

Book design by Penny & Tony Mills
Cover design by Sutchinda Rangsi Thompson

Cover images (front, top): *Images from the Tortoiseshell Butterfly project*. Photo by Simon Winnall.
Cover images (front, below): **Sheep** *by Thomas Hill, 2006. Steel wire, steel sheet. Dimensions: 61 x 46 x 25.5cm (24 x 18 x 10in) each.*

Cover images (back): **Neil's Shoes** *by Cathy Miles, 2007.* **Seated Figure** *by Rachel Ducker, 2008.*

Printed and bound in China

This book is produced using paper that is made from wood grown in managed, sustainable forests. It is natural, renewable and recyclable. The logging and manufacturing processes conform to the environmental regulations of the country of origin.

INTRODUCTION

In this book I would like to share some of the joy that working with wire has given me. The material has an amazing ability to capture the excitement and energy within the making process, each sculpture taking on the personality of its creator. Even someone who has never worked with metal before will achieve something very quickly, as wire sculptures can be made at the most basic level, even with just your fingers. Many wire sculptures are like three-dimensional drawings; they have a wonderful airy presence, containing space and casting dramatic shadows when placed in directed light. In a way, your pair of pliers or your fingers are like the pen and the wire is like the ink. The process is very similar in thought pattern to drawing, but wire allows you to achieve depth , which creates an exciting two- and three-dimensional quality that changes depending on where you view it from and what light you position it in.

You need very few tools to give wire sculpture a try. Those you do need are widely available from DIY or hobby shops. The book starts with a project that uses pliers, a fundamental tool throughout. It demonstrates that with just a few bends in the right places a sculpture can be made with very little equipment and fuss. Throughout the other four practical projects the level of technical difficulty increases in complexity, detail, design and use of additional materials. These projects should give you a good feel for the material and will give you the basic skills needed to pursue sculptures and subjects that interest you. Most of the projects work on a reasonably small scale so that you can get used to it; once you have the necessary skills you can easily scale up using thicker gauges of wire.

The last chapter gives you the option of taking your skills on to the next level. There are various ways of joining wire other than using the wire itself: using lead solder, a laser welder or a spot-welder, for example. This project demonstrates the use of silver soldering, a process commonly used in the jewellery and silversmithing industries. Silver-soldering techniques represent a jump up in difficulty, so this project is an introduction. It is worth bearing in mind that there are health and safety issues when soldering, as you are dealing with high heat, and the process does require a few more tools than you would get from your standard DIY shop. If you want to keep the number of tools to a minimum, or maybe don't feel confident using a gas blowtorch, the project can still be done using the techniques acquired through the previous projects.

Wire is a common, everyday material, normally associated with DIY repairs or farming. However, within sculpture it can be used in a variety of ways in terms of different techniques and aesthetics. I hope that this book demonstrates the fantastic diversity of wire sculpture that is being made out there through the different projects and in the images of others' creations. Perhaps you will draw inspiration from this and adopt your own style. Do have fun giving these projects a go, and remember that nothing has to be perfect – even the roughest drawings have a lively spirit, so cultivate and celebrate this!

(Opposite) **Sitting Figure** *by Rachel Ducker, 2007. Body from annealed steel wire, with lead sheet feet. Ht (approx.): 45cm (17¾ in.).* Photo courtesy of artist.

CHAPTER 1

GETTING STARTED

INSPIRATION

Starting a sculpture can sometimes be the trickiest part of the process. Although this book provides structured projects for you to try, I think it is worth talking in brief about conceiving ideas, as this is a valuable tool for future projects you may wish to try on your own.

Who knows where ideas come from; sometimes they are instant, like a brilliant thunderbolt, and at other times they are painful and difficult, as if one were attempting to draw blood from a stone. I believe ideas should have as much opportunity as possible. You have to open your mind up to possibility and create fodder on which your creative brain can feast. Day trips are always good, you may decide to look at nature, visit a place of architectural interest or just eavesdrop in a café! Whatever it is, take a sketchbook with you in case a gem of an idea twinkles at you; it may be a physical form or even a seed of a story.

When you have an idea, you need to shape it and make a series of decisions and experiments to make it work. The creative process is all about going back and forth with ideas; slowly you will hone them down to what you actually want from the piece. To help with these decisions I think it is a good idea to collect as much secondary information as possible to inform your sculpture. For example, if you want to make a bird, go and look at them in the wild, take photos and pore through nature books and magazines to collect images for reference. Which species do you want to portray? Do you want to do something realistic and structured or do you want to do an abstract sculpture concentrating on capturing the essence of a bird?

When you have decided on your approach, use drawing as a method of gaining a greater insight into your subject. It will help to inform your sculpture as drawing forces you to look very carefully at something, taking in its proportion and what makes up its essence. Developing a sound drawing skill is a really useful tool for pursuing sculpture. I spent about six years regularly attending life-drawing classes; I thoroughly recommend them for developing an artistic eye. Practice will teach you how to look at subjects properly; it will also help to develop confidence as you learn to free up.

It is usual during the design process, when using other sculptural materials, to make models to resolve the problems that arise when converting something from 2D to 3D. However, because wire sculpture tends to hover somewhere between drawing and three dimensions, I believe it is better to work straight into the wire to resolve any problems; this keeps energy within the piece. Wire is plentiful; there is no need to be careful about how much you use, so why would you need to work with any other material? When I was studying for my degree in silversmithing and jewellery, I often made models in wire before making my final piece in metal. I always found that my models had far more life and were much better pieces than my final ones in metal. Working straight into wire keeps the piece lively and spontaneous. Some sculptors do wire studies of their subjects on location to inform a larger piece, but they are beautiful pieces in their own right.

Study of a Walking Whooper Swan *by Celia Smith, 2007. Copper wire, telephone cabling and spray paint. Height: 22cm (8 ⅝in.).*
'This study was made whilst on a residency at the WWT centre in Welney, Norfolk. Through making this study I was able to understand more about how the swans walked on land. I saw it very much as a 3D drawing.'
Photo by Peter Stone.

WIRE

There are many different types of wire available of all gauges and properties. In the UK, the gauge of wire is usually measured in millimetres. You can get wire as fine as 0.05mm (US gauge 16) going up to as thick as 4mm (US gauge 6). The gauge of wire you use can often dictate the scale that you work at, naturally the bigger the gauge of wire the larger the piece. Really fine wire is great for jewellery and perhaps for finer detail within sculpture. It may be used for wire-knitted sculptural pieces because it resembles thread. Any wire over 0.7mm (US gauge 21) is good for creating wire structures for sculpture. My favourite gauge is 1mm (US gauge 18) because it has enough strength to keep itself upright, yet enough flexibility to capture detail. Wire between 2–3mm (US 12–8) is good for adding a strong defined line. It is also useful structurally when scaling up, as it can sustain more weight.

There is a huge variety of wire out there, from telephone-cable wire you find on the street to platinum wire for constructing the most expensive jewellery. Apart from being different in appearance they also have different properties and will therefore feel different to work with. They each have disadvantages and advantages which I have listed opposite. When you know a bit more about the properties of each metal then it is easier to make a more informed decision as to which one to use. My favourite wire, which I use throughout the book, is iron wire or black annealed steel wire, as it is sometimes known. It has a great quality for drawing with, as it is easily manipulated yet has the strength to stay in place after you have bent it, unlike some of the other softer metals such as copper, which can easily alter its shape after you have worked on it.

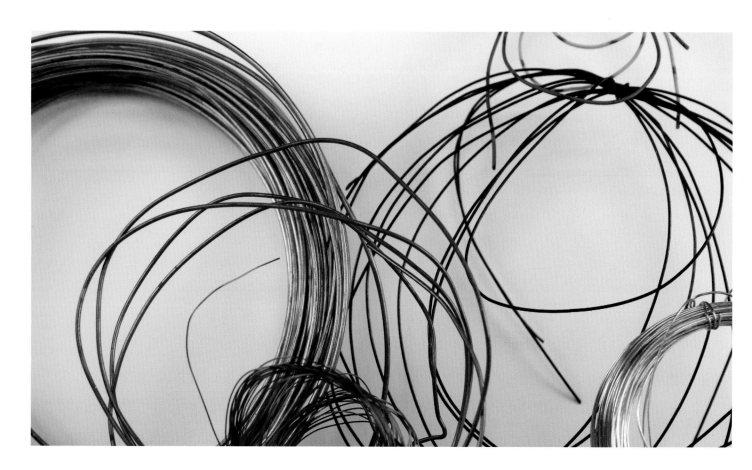

Type of Wire	Advantages	Disadvantages
IRON WIRE / BLACK ANNEALED STEEL WIRE	• Great to draw with, easy to manipulate yet will stay in the desired shape due to its natural strength. • It is versatile because it can be both spot-welded and soldered when using the appropriate solders and fluxes.	• Will rust in its natural state and therefore isn't appropriate for outside use. However, you can buy a galvanised version that is able to withstand the elements.
STAINLESS STEEL WIRE	• Has a wonderful springy quality creating movement in a sculpture. • Has hygienic qualities. • Can be spot- or laser-welded.	• Very tough to manipulate, it springs back on you, and is difficult to control!
COPPER WIRE	• Easily manipulated and can be silver-soldered. • Can be used outdoors as it doesn't rust.	• It is very soft and may change shape and distort after manipulation, especially after soldering.
BRASS WIRE	• Can be silver-soldered. • Can be used outdoors as it doesn't rust.	• It's quite a hard metal and therefore not the easiest to manipulate.
ALUMINIUM	• Nice and soft, easy to manipulate. • Can be used outside and doesn't really discolour, unlike brass, copper and silver.	• Has a very low melting point therefore can't be soldered. You can only bind or twist with it.
SILVER	• A very beautiful metal that is easy to manipulate. • Can be silver-soldered.	• Very expensive. • Like copper it can be quite soft so can misshape, especially after soldering.

(Opposite page) *Different types of wire. From left to right: brass wire, copper wire, red-coloured copper wire, iron wire, silver wire.*

COLOURED WIRE

There are also a variety of coloured wires, for example, enamelled and plated copper wire and anodised aluminium wire. These, however, can only be used during binding, twisting and knitting, as any applied heat would destroy the colourful surface. There are also wires that have been coated in cotton or plastic (like telephone wire). These are also sensitive to heat, so again you are restricted as to how you use them, but they are great for adding detail and creating extra texture.

WIRE MESH

There is also a variety of wire meshes you could use; they are good for creating 'fuller' sculptures. You could use aviary wire to create larger sculptures (**but be very careful not to cut yourself, gloves and goggles are required**) or annealed copper-wire mesh that comes in a variety of different thicknesses of weave and colour. Wire mesh is something you could keep a look out for if you are a thrifty scrap hunter; it has many different applications especially in the building trade.

All the projects in this book, with the exception of the last aeroplane project, can be made with most wires. You can follow them as closely as you want to. There is a comprehensive list of suppliers at the back of the book if you would like to buy the same wires described in each project. However, you can also use whichever wires come to hand. For example, you may find some fencing wire in the local DIY shop, or you may come across some reclaimed copper wire. The wire doesn't have to be the exact gauge stated in the materials list, you just need to get it as close as you can.

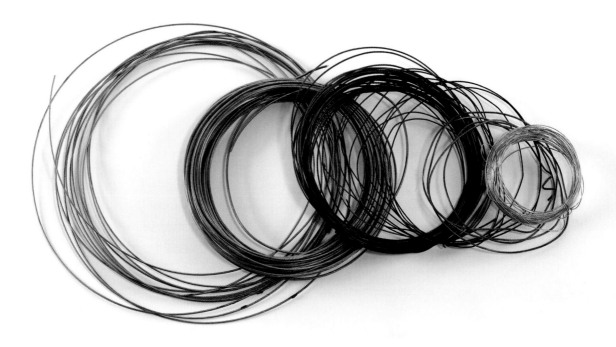

EQUIPMENT AND TOOLS

First things first: where are you going to work?

Ideally, the space should be clutter-free and the floor should be a hard surface rather than carpeted. This is because you don't want to lose sharp snippets of wire in your carpet or worse still drop red-hot wires!

BENCH

You don't need an amazing workshop when you start making wire sculptures, but there are a couple of essentials that will really help. Firstly, you need a workbench. This doesn't need to be too fancy but it does need to be sturdy. An old wooden table is fine, but you may need to attach it to the wall with brackets as you don't want it to wobble about whilst you are working, especially when using the vice.

Secondly, you need good light, as working with small pieces of wire can be hard on the eyes. I recommend getting a desk lamp and replacing the normal bulb with a daylight bulb; other natural light is also an advantage.

Next, a vice is useful for straightening wire. Because we won't be doing particularly heavy work, I recommend getting a hobby vice, which is a small version of the standard vice. This is good because you can just clamp it to the bench and it is movable. The other option is to use a metalworking vice. This is also bolted onto the bench so is immovable. It is bigger with larger jaws, so is useful if you want to work with larger-gauge wire.

(Opposite) *Bundles of wire.*

HAND TOOLS

To follow the projects in this book you won't need an abundance of tools, but there are a few staples that we will use regularly. These are pliers, wire cutters and tin snips. There are different versions of these, so I have provided some information on which ones we will use and what each one does. Don't be put off by this list as you can get by with a pair of pliers and a pair of snips. I'm sure that you will find a pair of pliers that you like and that feel right. You don't always have to buy brand new; keep an eye out at car-boot sales as they often have a wealth of unusual tools.

WIRE CUTTERS

These are indispensable for cutting wire. They are widely available in DIY and jewellery tool shops. The ones you see here are the ones that I use; they're called side cutters. These don't cut the wire so that the end is precisely flat; instead they cut it into a rough point. This is fine for the sculpture we will be making, as we shall not need to rely on flat ends.

If you are repeatedly cutting hard wires such as steel or iron then you may find that the cutters become blunt more easily and need to be replaced. They will probably struggle with wire over 2mm (US gauge 12).

TIN SNIPS

Also called straight shears, these are good for cutting very thin metal sheet such as found tin. They are also needed to cut small pallions of silver solder. Do not use them for cutting wire though, or you will blunt them. You may be able to get them from a DIY shop, but a jewellery tool supplier will definitely have them.

From left to right: flat-nose pliers, household pliers, snipe-nose pliers, wire cutters, tin snips/shears.

SNIPE-NOSE PLIERS

These are my most useful pair of pliers. They have jaws that taper to a point but are flat inside. Because of the narrow point and flat interior you have a lot of control, which is good for creating fine detail and getting into tight spaces. They are also very good for binding wire together, as the specific points allow you to apply pressure in the right places and the flat inside allows you to grip with ease. You can get these from a hobby shop or jewellery tool supplier.

HOUSEHOLD PLIERS

These you can definitely get from a DIY shop. They look like a bigger version of the snipe-nose pliers, but have grips running along the inside. These grips are a blessing and a curse. Good if you want to grip something and need to apply a bit of force. Bad if you are using soft metals like copper because the grips will mark the metal. I refer to these as my 'desert island pliers' as they are a good all-rounder. If you are just starting out and only want to invest in a cheap pair or happen to have one in the tool cupboard, then give these a go. The other plus is that they have a small wire cutter in the middle. Not the best wire cutter you will ever use, but good in a wire emergency!

FLAT-NOSE PLIERS

The jaws of these pliers are smooth and flat. You will find them in jewellery tool suppliers. They are great for straightening out kinks in wire and making sharp right-angled bends because of the larger flat jaws. They are not so great for doing detailed pattern, because you can't get in to small spaces.

SAFETY GOGGLES

Although not really a hand tool, this is a very useful and necessary piece of equipment. They are essential when soldering, as you need to protect your eyes from any debris or flux that may fly off during the soldering process. They are also useful when doing general wirework to protect your eyes from any stray wire ends, which you don't want flicking up into your eyes. They are available from DIY shops; make sure to get a comfortable pair, which are made of an unbreakable material.

ARALDITE GLUE

Again, although not strictly a hand tool, Araldite is a very strong two-part epoxy-resin glue which can be used on a wide variety of materials. The resin and the hardener need to be mixed in equal quantities to achieve a good result. This is very useful for securing other materials to the wire such as beads or fabric. Sometimes the wire itself will hold these materials but putting a little bit of glue in the right place will make the structure even more secure.

WORKING GLOVES

A pair of heavy-duty gloves is useful when cutting tin with shears. They will prevent you from cutting your hands on the sharp edges. You can pick up a pair from your local DIY shop.

OTHER MATERIALS

Most of the projects in this book include other materials to inject colour, suggest solidity in places, or give different textures. I suggest you keep an eye out for different materials to use for your own sculptures. For the projects in this book, I have used found items, from fake flowers through to fishing flies. Old biscuit tins are always useful as they are an easy way to add life and colour, as are found pieces of coloured cardboard and tissue paper, or even newspaper. Utilising reclaimed materials such as these may add narrative and spark inspiration as you discover found imagery or text within them. You may also find old bits of textile you want to use, perhaps from old clothes or a handbag. Beads and old buttons are useful for small details in sculptures, or perhaps you could take an element from an old plastic toy. Feathers are another way of introducing colour and texture; fishing shops are a good source for these. It's a good idea to visit charity shops and car-boot sales for random materials. You never know what you may find, which adds to the fun.

SOLDERING EQUIPMENT

If you want to take wire sculpture a step further, silver soldering is a good way to create strong neat joins between wires. This will enable you to join wires in awkward-to-reach spots where you may not be able to use binding or twisting techniques. The soldering process uses solder to fill in the joins, in this case silver solder, which has a high silver content. Many metals can be silver-soldered including silver, copper, brass, and gilding metal. The metal join you want to solder needs to be cleaned, and both surfaces have to be touching each other fully. A flux is then applied around the joint to keep the surface clean. Solder is then placed on the join and heat is applied using a gas torch. This heat then melts the solder and the join filled. After soldering you must remove excess flux. This is usually done by placing the join in a warm cleaning solution called pickle, which also removes any oxide; but we are not really bothered about the oxide, so we will just use hot soapy water and a brush.

This is an outline of the equipment you will need. As I said in the introduction, you will have to get these tools from a jewellery tool supplier as they are more specialist. There is a list of suppliers at the back of the book (see p.94–5).

HANDHELD BUTANE GAS TORCH

To provide heat, you will need a blowtorch. This device mixes air and propane to create heat. The one I recommend for beginners is the handheld butane version. It is quite gentle and the butane is easily available from newsagents (it's the gas you use to refill lighters). It is not great for working with thick wire or larger-scale work; for that you need more heat, i.e. a big gas torch connected directly to a bottle of gas via a hose. However, for our purposes, a small handheld version will be fine. The butane is stored in the handle; on the base of the torch you will find a little hole, which is where you place the nozzle of the butane refill and press down to release the gas into the chamber. In the nozzle of the torch there are holes that draw an air supply, which is controlled through a dial. This changes the type of flame generated and therefore the type of heat. You can get these from DIY shops but I would recommend buying it from a jewellery tool supplier as they can also answer any questions you may have, especially if you are soldering for the first time.

SOLDERING BLOCK

It is important to solder on a heatproof material, and these specially designed soldering blocks (see opposite) are great. They come in different sizes and thicknesses. I went for a large block, which is good for sculpture as we will be dealing with bigger objects and it would be annoying if the work fell off the block during the soldering process because the block was too small! Soldering blocks can be bought from jewellery tool suppliers.

BORAX CONE AND DISH

Borax is the flux we will be using. Flux prevents dirty oxide from building up when applying heat. We need it because solder relies on clean surfaces in order to flow. Borax comes in a solid cone that you grind up in a borax dish with water to make a milky paste. The borax is applied to the joins with a brush. You can get your borax cone and dish from jewellery tool suppliers.

SILVER SOLDER

Silver solder comes in three different grades – hard, medium and easy. We will be using easy solder as it has the lowest melting point: it requires less heat to melt it, unlike hard solder which, although stronger, requires a greater amount of heat. Solder comes in single strips that are cut into small squares called pallions. Use your tin snips or shears to cut vertical lines about 1mm (less than $\frac{1}{16}$ in.) apart at the end of the stick of solder, only do about 1cm ($\frac{3}{8}$ in.) long cuts. Then cut horizontally,

Soldering equipment. From left to right: borax cone and dish, butane gas torch, stainless-steel tweezers, reverse-action tweezers, strip of easy solder, all placed on top of soldering block.

keeping one finger at the end of the stick to support any falling pallions as they are cut. Cut every 1–2mm (approx. ⅟₁₆in.) to keep them small. As you cut pop them into your borax dish to keep them clean. Silver solder is again available at jewellery tool suppliers.

REVERSE-ACTION TWEEZERS WITH INSULATED HANDLES

These are great for gripping work and keeping your piece in position whilst soldering; they are like an extra pair of fingers! You may want to get two pairs as they are very useful. They are available from jewellery tool suppliers.

STAINLESS-STEEL TWEEZERS

These have a very fine point and are excellent for picking up pallions of solder to put along the joint ready for soldering. They are also useful during the soldering process as you can use them to reposition any pallions or pieces of metal that have shifted position during soldering. Remember, the metal gets very hot. You don't want to use your fingers for this; that's what pliers are for. I still occasionally forget that wire gets hot after soldering, and I have achieved nice wire imprints running along my palm on many occasions from picking up the wire too quickly!

BRUSH

When cleaning off the excess borax in soapy water, it is a good idea to have a small brush to hand to get at the joins and give them a good scrub. You can use an old toothbrush or bottlebrush.

BASIC TECHNIQUES

Now you know about the tools that are useful for wire sculpture and have found out a little bit about their application, it's time to look at preparation and basic wire techniques which will help you to complete the projects in this book.

PREPARATION

First of all you need to look at the wire you will be using and decide whether it needs any preparation before you use it for sculpture. Sometimes wire can be coated in oil or grease to protect it from the elements. In the case of iron wire this is very common as the oil prevents rust. We need to remove this grease. To do that, reel a good amount off the spool of wire and cut with the wire cutters.

Next take the end of the wire and with your flat-nose pliers bend the end over by about 0.5cm (⅜ in.) so there is no longer a sharp point but a blunt point. Repeat this at the other end. This minimises the risk of you cutting your hands whilst washing the wire, as the ends can be quite sharp.

Next you need a washing-up bowl of hot soapy water and some Fairy Liquid. Try to keep the wire together in a rough circle and dip it in the water. Put some neat Fairy Liquid over the wire and rub in between your hands to develop a good lather, then wash away the suds in the hot water. You may need to do this a couple of times if the wire is really greasy.

If you are using a metal such as brass, copper or gilding metal and want to solder it, then you must remove any trace of grease, otherwise soldering will not work. Although these wires are less likely to be coated in oil than iron wire often is, it is a good idea to run some sandpaper or a piece of kitchen scourer along the length of the wire to make sure it is pristine.

You may find that if the wire you are using has been taken off a tightly packed spool, it has kept a circular shape. Working with circular wire is a pain, so it is useful to know how to straighten it. To do this cut a length of wire, anything up to 1–2 metres (3–6 feet). Put one end of the wire in a vice and tighten it really well. Grip the other end with your pair of household pliers (make sure the pliers have grips running along the inside) and pull the wire quite hard, so it's under tension. This will straighten the wire; you will also see the wire stretch a little and become slightly thinner in gauge. I tend to do a batch of wire straightening at a time so I don't have to repeat the process too often. It is also helpful to do this if the wire becomes kinked and bent, making it reusable.

BASIC WIRE MANIPULATION

Before launching into the projects you may like to try out some of these exercises, which will help you get used to the pliers. It is also a good opportunity to collect a couple of lengths of different wires – for example – iron, copper, brass, maybe stainless steel, to see how each one reacts. This will allow you to get to know the different metals and how they feel. You can also try different gauges of wire as each will have different visual effects and will require different levels of force with the pliers. I would recommend trying first with iron or copper.

ZIGZAG PATTERN

This is a good exercise to get you used to bending with pliers, a fundamental skill for wire sculpture. First of all cut several 30cm (12in.) lengths of wire. Next take a pair of snipe nose pliers in one hand and in the other hand hold the end of the wire between your forefinger and thumb. Grab the wire in the pliers beside your fingers and bend upwards. Then reposition

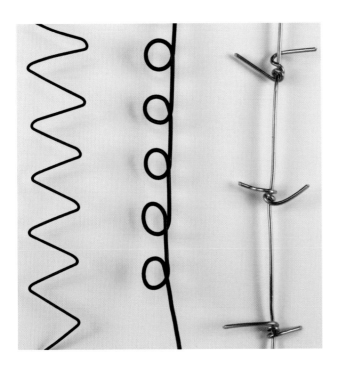

your forefinger and thumb along the long end of wire about 1–2cm (⅜–¾ in.) from the first bend and bend back downwards. Repeat this movement, creating a series of zigzags. When you have finished try another length, this time using the flat-nose pliers, then another length using the household pliers. This will help you to get a better feel for the different pliers and what each one can do.

LENGTH OF CIRCLES

Take another length of wire (again experiment with different metals and gauges). As before, take your snipe-nose pliers in one hand and hold the end of the wire between your forefinger and thumb. Grip the wire with the pliers near your fingers and start to guide the wire downwards into a small circle. When you reach a half-circle, you may want to use your thumb to gently guide the wire back upwards. Bring it all the way around until it crosses the start of the circle, then place the pliers with one jaw inside the circle and the other jaw outside at the top of the circle. Then squeeze, so that the wires touch each other neatly at the top of the circle, keeping the long end straight so you can make the next circle. Repeat this until you have a line of circles. Circles are required in some of the projects to make eyes, heads, feet and other decoration; it is a useful shape to get the hang of.

(Opposite) *From left to right: zigzag, length of circles, joining with binding.*

JOINING WITH BINDING

Nearly all the projects in this book use binding as a method to join two wires. To practise this technique, we are going to make a length of barbed wire. Start with a length of 30cm (12in.) wire and cut several 5cm (2in.) lengths. You may want to use 1mm gauge (US gauge 18) wire for this, as you may find it an easier gauge to work with. Hold the 30cm (12in.) length of wire in between your forefinger and thumb and place a short 5cm ((2in.) length across it (so it looks like a cross). Hold in position with your forefingers, keeping one short end steady whilst bending the other short end around the 30cm (12in.) length. Bind it round the wire two or three times and then get a pair of snipe-nose pliers (or household pliers if you need a better grip) and squeeze around the binds until the two wires are so tightly pressed together that they no longer move. You may find that if you squeeze in a couple of different places along the bind – for example, the front, back and sides – then you may get a tighter join. Practice this along the whole length of the 30cm (12in.) wire so you will find it easier to do in the projects when you have to do binds in specific places.

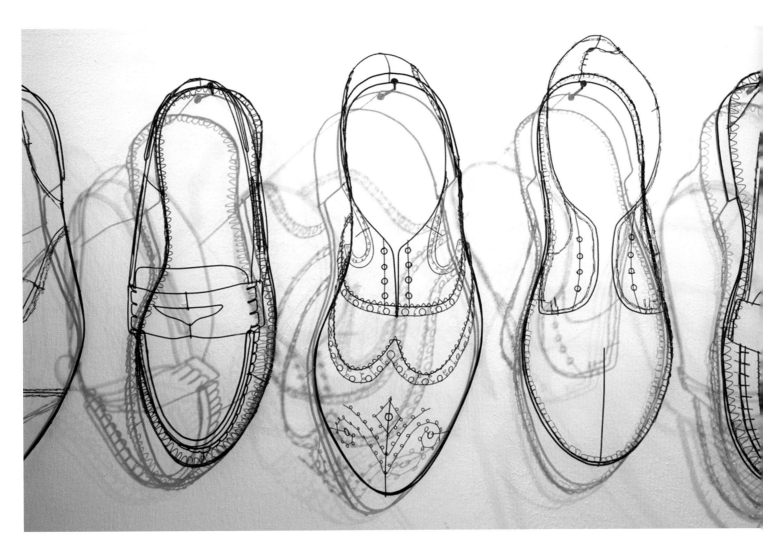

Neil's Shoes *by Cathy Miles, 2007. Spot-welded iron wire manipulated with pliers. Life-size.*
'Inspiration for these shoes is taken from a silversmith called Neil. Neil brings his old shoes into work to spend their retirement period as work shoes. When they can work no more they end up in the workshop shoe pile, each shoe a little different, but the same.' Photo courtesy of artist.

(Opposite) Perch Piece *by Thomas Hill, 2007. Mild steel wire, dimensions: 640 x 970 x 280cm (252 x 382 x 110in.).* Photo courtesy of artist.

CHAPTER 2

THE PELICAN

This little pelican can be made using a couple of simple techniques. Colour is incorporated using coated copper wire for the body and a bright found mustard tin for the beak. This project primarily concentrates on practising bending wire with snipe-nosed pliers, creating shapes, which allows the personality of the pelican to develop. This sculpture was inspired by a trip to St James's Park in London; the resident Pelican there doesn't look like the sharpest tool in the box!

For this project you will need a spool of coated copper wire. As this comes in a huge array of colours, you can have fun choosing which one to use; however, here a golden yellow has been chosen to complement the found tin. The wire comes in a variety of thicknesses; again you have freedom to choose, though I would recommend you use any between 0.3mm–0.5mm (US gauges 28–24). Some black iron wire is also required. Here 0.9mm (US gauge 19) has been used, which is a good thickness to use when drawing with wire for the first time. You will also need a found tin for the beak, preferably in yellow, and a paintbrush for the tail. The paintbrush used here has some colour variation in the bristles; it is worth keeping an eye out for one with character. As for tools, you will need snipe-nose pliers, household pliers, wire cutters, snips, scissors and some Araldite glue.

MATERIALS

- Colour-coated copper wire
- Black iron wire or black annealed steel wire (1mm gauge/US gauge 18)
- Mustard tin or other yellow tin
- Emulsion paintbrushes

Tools

- Snipe-nose pliers
- Household pliers
- Wire cutters
- Tin snips/shears
- Scissors
- Araldite glue

Finished pelicans. Dimensions approx. 10 x 8cm (4 x 3in.).

Photo courtesy of author.

Lightly roll copper in between the palms of the hands to form a ball.

Bend iron wire at a right angle.

Start by unravelling a decent amount of copper wire from the spool; don't be too mean with it, as you want a large ball to play with. You can mix different colours of wire if you like. Cut the wire with wire cutters and start to gently roll it to form a ball in the palms of your hands. Be gentle, otherwise you will squash the ball; you may want to stretch it out and roll it back up again to redistribute the wire to make a more even ball.

Next, start making the feet and a holder for the body. To do this, get a piece of straight iron wire about 70cm (27in.) long. Take the snipe-nose pliers and bend the wire about 20cm (8in.) from the end of the wire at a right angle. If you use the tip of the pliers, you will get more control over the wire.

This bent shorter portion of the wire is the start of a foot. Next, make a toe by bending the wire left 3cm (1¼ in.) from the first bend; then bend it back down on itself and up again to create a V. Then bend the wire left again to create the second toe and bend it back down again so the wire ends up near the first right-angle bend, then cut any excess wire.

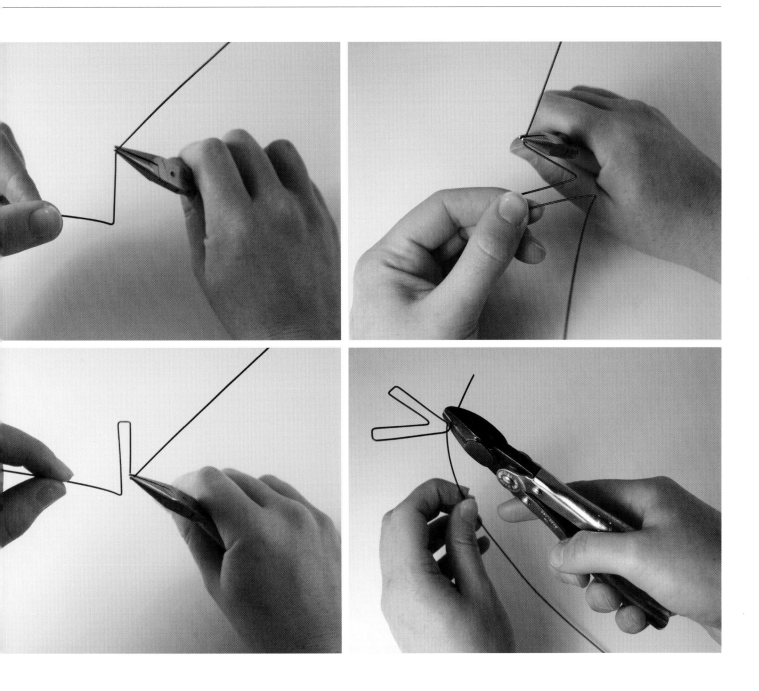

(Top) *Bend left to create start of toe.*

(Above) *Bend wire downwards and then back up to create a V.*

(Top) *Bend left again to create second toe. Bend back down again towards the longer end of wire and cut off excess.*

(Above) *Cut excess wire from foot, keeping the longer end intact.*

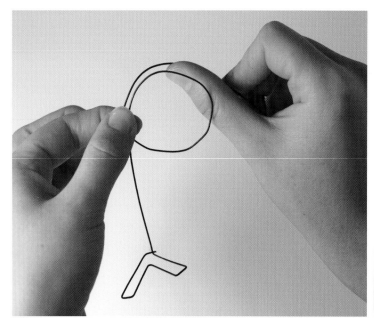

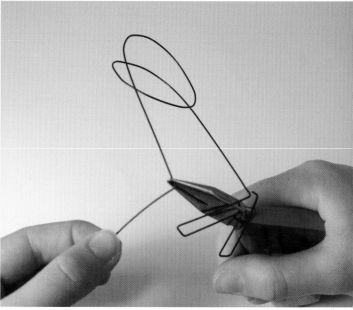

Bend wire into a circle using fingers and back around so it is parallel to the first foot.

Bend wire at right angles in the same place as the other foot.

Next, pick up the wire so the toes are pointing towards you and the long wire is in your right hand. You need to make a circular holder for the wire ball to fit into, so with your fingers start to bend the long wire into a circle. The wire should end up parallel to the first foot. Make the circle slightly smaller than the size of the wire ball.

Now repeat the process of making the first foot using the long portion of wire to make the second foot and leg. Try to make sure that you bend the wire at right angles in the same place as the other foot so that both feet will be at the same height.

Repeat the same steps to make the toes as you did on the first foot, cutting off any excess wire you might have when finished. Next place the feet on the work surface, holding them down with one hand. Use your other hand to gently move the circle backwards and forwards to encourage the frame to stand. This will require some trial and error, but with practice it will balance!

When the frame is standing, place the wire ball through the circle and very gently squeeze the iron wire circle to create a snug fit.

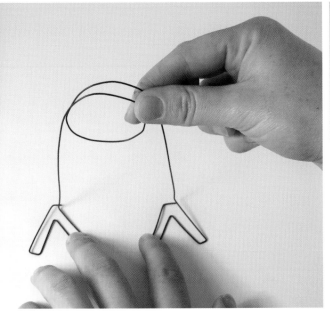

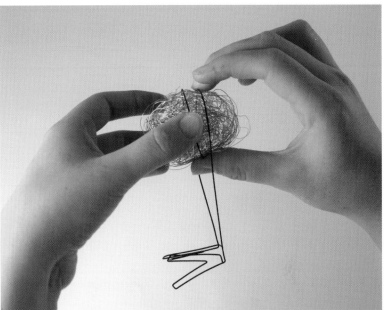

(Above) *Gently move the circle backwards and forwards by holding down the legs until the frame is balanced and standing.*
(Above right) *Place the wire ball through circle and gently squeeze the iron wire for a snug fit.*
(Right) *Use the snipe-nose pliers to bind the iron wire around the bristles.*

Next, cut a pinch of bristles from the paintbrush and get a 40cm (15¾ in.) length of 0.9mm (US gauge 19) iron wire. Keeping the bristles together with your thumb and forefinger, take the iron wire and using the snipe-nose pliers bind it around the end of the bristles a couple of times to keep them all together. You may want to use the household pliers to squeeze the wire tightly to make sure none of the bristles fall out.

Place the wire with bristles through the copper-wire body.

Bend the wire around the body.

Bend the iron wire so it is in line with the bristles, and place it through the copper-wire ball so the bristles form a tail.

Use the snipe-nose pliers to bend the iron wire around the underneath of the body so that it goes round past the tail and back up to the front of the body.

At this point bend the wire upwards to create a neck. At about 4cm (1½in.) along the neck start to bend the wire, using the snipe nose pliers, to form a circle. Keep bending the wire around until you have a double circle and the long end of the wire ends up towards the feet. Cut off the excess. Make sure that the two wires running parallel to each other which make up the head are

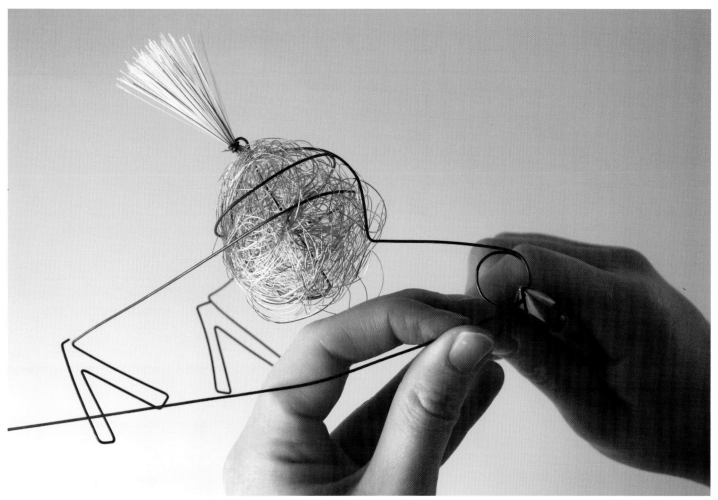

(Above) *Using snipe-nose pliers, bend wire around in a double circle to form the head. The excess wire should end up by the feet.*
(Right) *Cutting out the beak using snips.*

touching in as many places as possible, as they will provide a holder for the beak. Using the tin snips, cut a rectangle out of the found tin, about 5 x 3cm (2 x 1¼in.). Then cut a beak shape out of this rectangle. Here you can use your imagination, as the beak shape really adds character. Before you cut, you can draw on the reverse side of the tin with permanent pen first if this helps.

Place the beak through the two wires making up the head.

Applying the Araldite glue.

Place the cut-out beak through the two parallel wires making up the head of the pelican. If the wires are close enough together they should hold the beak in position.

Mix up some Araldite glue and place a dab at the back of the beak where it touches the wire. Allow to dry; this usually takes about half an hour with the quick-drying type.

Your pelican is now finished. You could make a few and create a flock; then stories can start to develop …

Stone Curlew by Cathy Miles, 2008.
Iron wire, spray paint, lavatory brush, tin. Height: 40cm (15¾in.).
Spot-welded and silver-soldered.
'I love to investigate the spatial trickery wire sculpture lends
itself to. One minute it looks 2D, then the shadows flood it
into glorious three dimensions before it's photographed and
placed in a book as an illustration.' Photo courtesy of artist.

(Left) **Sheep** *by Thomas Hill, 2006. Steel wire, steel sheet.*

Dimensions: 61 x 46 x 25cm (24 x 18 x 10 in.) each.

'I make a simple sheep form from wire, then make the "wool" from thinner wire, gradually building up a flat sheet,
which gets soldered together, hammered flat, then shaped around the form to make the sheep look nice and woolly.
I was inspired by Henry Moore's sheep drawings in ballpoint pen and made my own drawn studies in pen to
work from.' Photo courtesy of Thomas Hill.

(Above) **The Guidance Session Rookery Nest** *by Cathy Miles, 2007.*
Iron wire, tin, brushes. Dimensions: 40 x 30cm (15 ¾ x 11 ¾in.).
Spot-welded and silver-soldered.
'The nest was mainly made with my bare hands; I wanted it to be free and expressive. Sometimes the best method of
achieving this is doing without pliers and their structural lines.'
Photo by Simon Winnall.

CHAPTER 3

TORTOISESHELL BUTTERFLY

The tortoiseshell butterfly is a tiny sculpture that I have adapted so it can be worn. I have used many found materials in this project, which I personally encourage as I think it can provide interesting textural contrasts. The beauty of it is that any materials that come to hand can be used. For this sculpture I raided a nature book, chose a species of butterfly I liked and then hunted and scavenged around for materials that reminded me of it in colour and texture. Fake flowers are good, old trimmings, anything like that is great. You can choose your favourite butterfly and mimic its patterns and shapes with the skills you learn in this project. A fishing fly is used to suggest the body. There are many varieties of fishing fly available (at the back of the book you will find some suppliers). The flies have such funny names: the particular fly I have used is called a 'green high rider', and I deliberately chose it because it resembles a flying insect. We will be concentrating on creating finer detail with wire in this project, through pattern, and we will be using the binding techniques highlighted in the section on Basic Wire Manipulation (see p.22).

MATERIALS

- Black or grey iron wire/black annealed steel wire – 0.7mm and 0.5mm gauge (US gauge 21 and 24)
- Orange fake flower (preferably lily-shaped)
- Patent black fabric or other shiny black material
- Brooch/badge pin
- Scraps of brown leather
- Fishing fly

TOOLS

- Snipe-nose pliers
- Wire cutters
- Scissors
- Araldite glue

Completed butterfly brooches. Dimensions: approx. 9 x 7cm (3 ½ x 2 ¾ in.).

Photo by Simon Winnall.

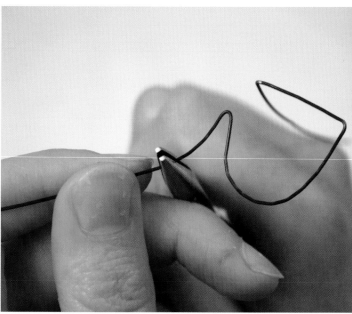

At 5cm (2in.) from the end, bend at right angles so the 5cm length of wire is facing downwards, then after 2cm (2in.) bend to your left.

Draw a curve for the lower wing and then bend back outwards to form the upper portion of the wing.

Again we will be using iron wire because it is tough but pliable. Start with approximately 1m (3ft) of 0.7mm (US gauge 21) iron wire. At about 5cm (2in.) in from one end, bend at right angles so the 5cm length of wire is facing downwards. Then after about 2cm (¾ in.) bend the wire to your left. I would recommend snipe-nose pliers for this job as they will give you control, especially when working small-scale.

Now start drawing the butterfly by drawing the bottom curve of the bottom portion of the wing. Then bend the wire back out again to form the larger upper portion of the wing.

Form the upper wing shape as in the photo, then curve the wire into the middle. Take your fishing fly, place in the middle and bind the wire around the top of the fishing fly.

Repeat the process on the other side to make up a similar set of wings.

I have based my wing shape on the tortoiseshell butterfly, but your butterfly may be different. You can follow the pattern in the next photo if you like. I made a couple of gentle bends and then brought the wire back towards the middle of the butterfly where I placed the first bend. Most fishing flies have a sharp hook which you will need to cut off, so take your chosen fishing fly and, using the wire cutters, cut off the hook from the main body of the fly so it does not get in the way. Be very careful doing this; wear goggles, and make sure nobody else is nearby: you don't want to get a fishing hook in your eye or theirs! Now place the fishing fly where the middle or body of the butterfly would be and bind the wire, making up the wing all the way around the top of the fishing fly so it ends up on the other side, ready to form the other wing. You may want to tighten the grip between the fishing fly and the wire by gently squeezing with some household pliers.

Repeat on the other side of the wing, trying to make the same bends in similar places. This may be a little tricky, as you are doing it by eye; and it may take some practice, but don't worry if it's not perfect, as this all adds to the character.

Bend the wire back towards the centre of the butterfly and then bind to the original downward-pointing wire.

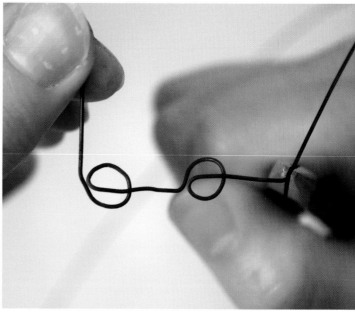

Bend wire into a small circle, leaving some excess to the left. Then run the wire through the middle of the circle and repeat until you have three circles. Then trim excess wire to your right-hand side.

When you have done this, bend the wire back towards the centre until you reach the original wire bending downwards. When you are there, bind the wire to this downward-pointing wire as the photo demonstrates.

When your wire butterfly outline is secure, it is time to make a start on the finer detail that will make up the pattern in the wings. To do this, get a 10cm (4in.) piece of 0.7mm (US gauge 21) iron wire and, starting at one end, form a small circle about half a centimetre wide. When the circle is formed bend the wire left so it goes through the circle, then make another circle about 1cm (⅜in.) from the previous circle. Repeat this pattern until you have three circles and then cut any excess wire from the right-hand side.

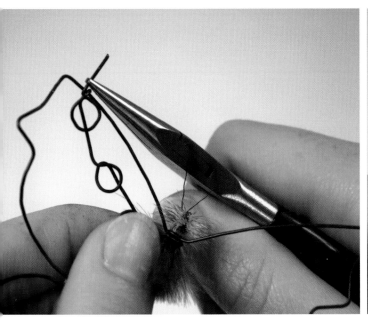

Bind the non-trimmed end of the length of circles to the top corner of each butterfly wing.

Create a series of joined up 'U's in the thinner 0.5mm wire.

Repeat this so you have a length of circles for one wing and another length for the other. Next, bind these circles to the butterfly wings. Use the end of wire you didn't trim off to bind to the top corner as shown in the photo, and repeat this process for each wing.

Now take 50cm (20in.) length or so of thinner, 0.5mm (US gauge 24), iron wire. This is a good thickness to get fine detail using the small pair of snipe-nose pliers. We need to create a pattern which is made up of a series of joined-up 'U's. With the pliers, form a little U-shape about half a centimetre tall and then turn the wire back down and gently squeeze with the pliers to get a point before forming another U. Repeat until you get a decent length – about 20–25cm (8–10in.) should do it, depending on the size of your butterfly.

(Above) *Bind detail to the top of the wing next to the circles. Run it down vertically, following the outline of the butterfly, finishing in the bottom corner, where it should then be bound to the wing again and any excess cut off.*
(Below) *Using your fake flower cut out the shapes as shown. Cut the shape in the middle out of a scrap of leather.*

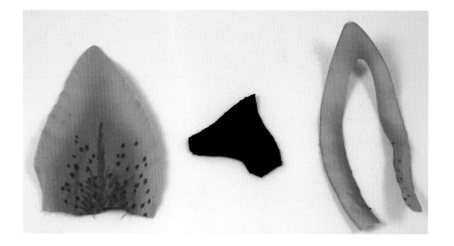

Now bind a length of this next to the circles you have just positioned, but this time run the detail vertically, following the outline of the wings, then bind into position at the end of the bottom wing. Cut any excess and repeat for the other wing.

Next take your fake flowers and scraps of leather and cut into butterfly wing shapes. You want one large colourful

Bind the textiles together with wire, placing the leather scrap in the middle. Then gently pull out the textiles, arranging in a suitable butterfly shape, and place this arrangement underneath one half of the wire butterfly frame.

piece cut into a point for the top wing. Then cut out a smaller, triangular-shaped piece in the leather, followed by another pointed shape in the fake flower (this time cut a hole in it as shown in the photo). These two pieces will make up the bottom wing.

Arrange the three pieces, making sure that the leather piece is placed in between the fake-flower scraps. Hold the pieces together with your forefingers and then get a little piece of the 0.7mm (US gauge 21) wire to bind the lot together, squeezing with the pliers to keep it in place. Make sure you have captured all the top ends of the material in the bind, as you don't want any escapee pieces! Also, don't trim any excess wire as you will need this shortly.

Now fan out the materials into position with your fingers, gently separating the large colourful pieces from the other two smaller pieces, which should sit on top of each other. When it looks right, slide your textile combination underneath one half of the wire butterfly wings. Once in the correct position, bind the textiles to the downward pointing wire in the middle of the butterfly.

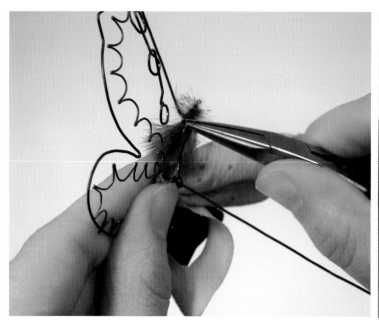

Once in the correct position bind the textiles to the downward-pointing wire that sits in the middle of the butterfly.

Carefully run a small amount of Araldite glue along the edge of the wire circles, then place a black patent circle over each wire circle, and allow to dry.
(Right) *Pull the downward wire through one of the holes in the flat plate and then bind around a couple of times before gluing with Araldite for extra stability.*

When it sits securely and you have made sure that the bind is tight, you may want to trim the textile shapes so that they fit nicely into the wire frame. Repeat the process for the other half, so both sides are filled with colour.

For the next stage take the piece of black patent material and cut out six circles, all slightly bigger than the wire circles you made a short while ago, which are attached to the butterfly. Mix up some Araldite glue and carefully place a small amount (you may want to use a wire scrap to do this) along the line of each circle. Then carefully place one black patent circle over each wire circle and allow to dry.

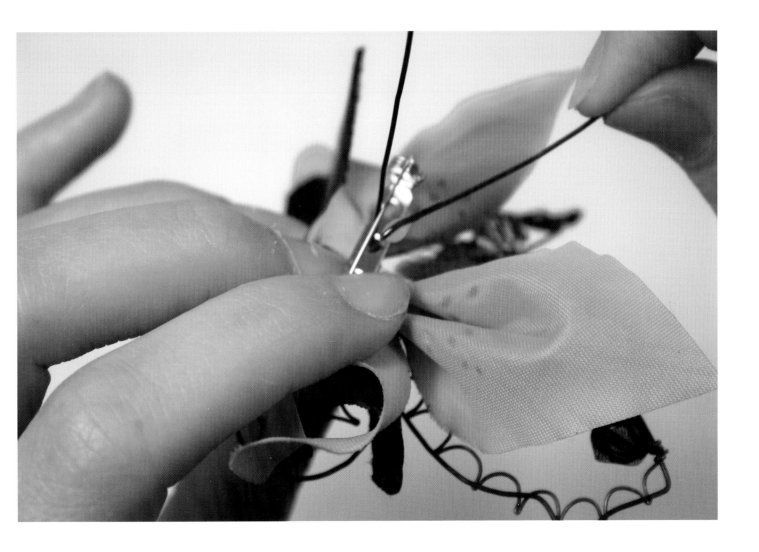

For the last step you will need the badge pin. Choose the sort with a pin connected to a flat plate with holes running through it, so that you can attach things to it. Place the wire that runs under the middle of the butterfly through one of these holes on the flat edge of the pin and pull it right through. Then bind around the flat edge a couple of times. While you are doing this, try to make sure that the pin is placed vertically along the butterfly to allow for better weight distribution. Squeeze the wire with household pliers to keep firmly in place and then mix up some Araldite glue and place in spots where the wire and flat plate meet.

Your tortoiseshell butterfly is now complete! If you are feeling particularly ambidextrous you could make the butterfly outline out of stainless-steel wire. This is much harder to work with because it is naturally springy. However, if you extended the downward wire that connects the butterfly to the brooch pin by about 5cm (2in.) say, the butterfly would then bob about because of its springy nature. Then your tortoiseshell could hover above your shoulder as if you were a sprig of lavender!

(Above) **Time for Tea** *by Priscilla Jones, 2006. Wire, acrylic paint, wax, printed silk, vintage buttons and lace.*
Dimensions: 38 x 23cm (15 x 9in.).
(Right) **Espresso Cups** *by Priscilla Jones, 2007. Wire, acrylic paint, wax, silk, vintage buttons and lace. Dimensions: 30 x 15cm (11¾ x 6in.).*
'I draw my inspiration from a variety of sources, exploring the concept of identity, memory and nostalgia; these themes underpin the
direction of my pieces. Hand-manipulated wire is used to create the structure of the piece, then the surface is worked through a process of
embellishment including hand and machine stitch on silk.'

Photos by Stephen Lamb.

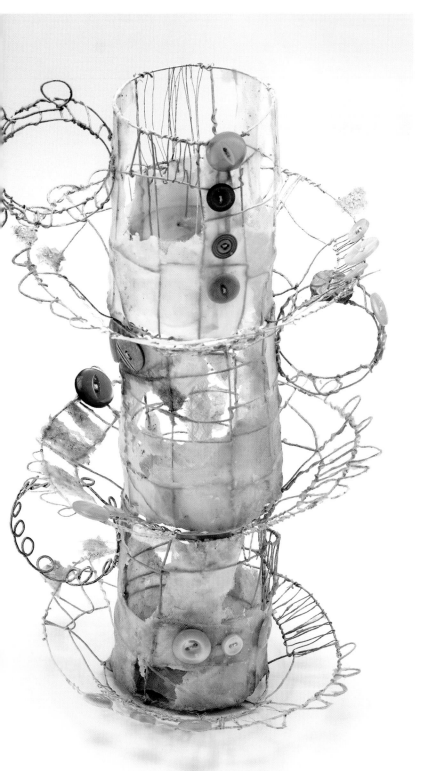

Sylvia *by Jayne Lennard.*
'It is the quality of decaying materials that fascinates, the richness of texture, a story already attached; it is then a matter of bringing these various objects together into a new whole. To reclaim is to see infinite variations.'

CHAPTER 4

THE CZECHOSLOVAKIAN TEAPOT

This teapot is made through recycling a Liquorice All-sorts tin, although any brightly coloured tin will do; you will need a few different colours though. I love drawing tea sets, I was attracted to this Czechoslovakian teapot because the lively pattern enabled me to suggest space and form without drawing many structural lines.

The project focuses on binding wire together to create a 'three-dimensional drawing' as well as using the wire as a frame to bend tin over (which is called tabbing tin). The use of tin introduces colour in the same fashion as colouring in a line drawing. As well as some brightly coloured tin you will also need some 1.2mm (US gauge 16) and 0.9mm (US gauge 19) iron wire, and a bright bead approximately 2.5cm (1in.) in diameter. It's fun to see how your own teapot will develop, as your own found materials will dictate its particular personality and style. Tabbing with found colourful tin is a good way to introduce solid colour to sculpture without using heat. As you gain experience in the future you may wish to solder sheet metal that you then colour with paint.

MATERIALS

- Black iron wire or black annealed steel wire (1.2mm and 0.7mm gauge)
- A variety of colourful biscuit/sweet tins
- Colourful bead approximately 2.5cm (1in.) in diameter

TOOLS

- Household pliers
- Snipe-nose pliers
- Flat-nose pliers
- Tin snips/shears
- Wire cutters

Finished teapot. Dimensions: 20 x 25cm (8 x 10in.).

Photo courtesy of the author.

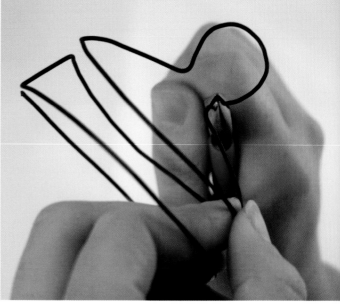

(Above left) *Bend the wire into a circle, then bend at a right angle upwards; then bend again at a right angle leaving a 1cm (⅜in.) gap.*

(Left) *Bend into a second slightly smaller circle and then bend the wire upwards towards the centre.*

(Above) *Bend upwards towards the middle to create a three-quarter circle, then bend the wire out across the middle of it.*

Start by taking a 50cm/20 in.(approx.) length of 1.2mm (US gauge 16) wire and bend it round in a circle approximately 9cm (3½ in.) wide. You can use your fingers to do this if you find it easier and then go around the circle with the flat-nose pliers to make it a more even circle, straightening out the dents with the pliers. When you have a circle you then need to bend the wire upwards to form a right angle, leaving a 1cm (⅜in.) gap bend at another right angle so that the wire is parallel with the circle.

Bend the parallel wire round into another circle slightly smaller than the original and bend the wire again at a right angle towards the centre of the circle.

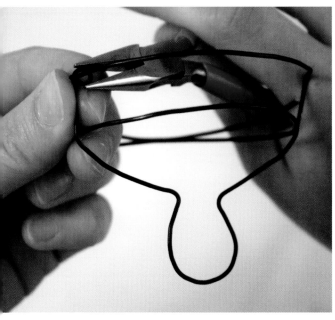

Wrap the wire once or twice around where the two wires meet on the original circle . Then squeeze with the household pliers for a tighter grip.

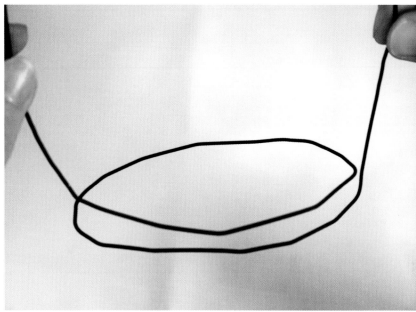

From the mid point of the wire bend into a 10cm (4in.) circle, making sure that the lengths of wire are opposite each other. Bend lengths upwards.

In the centre of the circle bend the wire upwards to form another small three-quarter circle. You should base this circle on the size of your bead, as it will act as a holder for the bead. Try to make the circle narrower at the base so that it will hold the bead properly. Then bend the wire back towards the other side of the circle.

Next, bend the wire back down towards the original circle and join here by wrapping the stray wire around the wire of the circle. Do this once or twice. Then use a pair of household pliers to squeeze the wrapped wire; this will achieve a tighter grip. Cut any remaining wire off with the wire cutters.

This is the teapot lid nearly completed. The next bit is the body. You will need approximately 1m (39in.) of 1.2mm (US gauge 16) wire. Find the midpoint of this wire and then draw a circle with your fingers/pliers approximately 10cm (4in.) in diameter. Go round with the wire until the two lengths of wire are opposite each other as in the photo. Bend these wires at right angles so they face upwards.

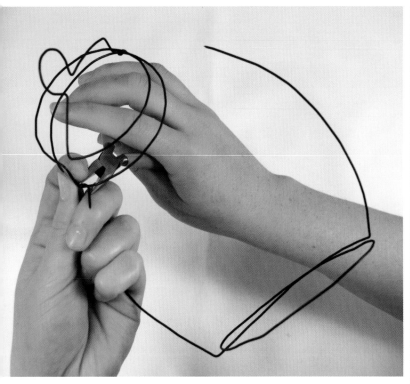

Join the teapot body to the lid by binding the length of wire around the bottom of the lid.

The lid is attached to the body by binding both sides.

Then gently curve these wires so that they form the bulbous sides of the teapot. When nicely curved trim the two lengths so they are about 12cm (4¾ in.) tall. Get the teapot lid and start to bind one length to the bottom wire of the lid, placing the bind next to the upright wire on the lid. Bind around just like the previous join, tightening again with the household pliers.

Do the same to the other length and attach to the opposite side of the circle.

Bend the wire into the following handle shape.

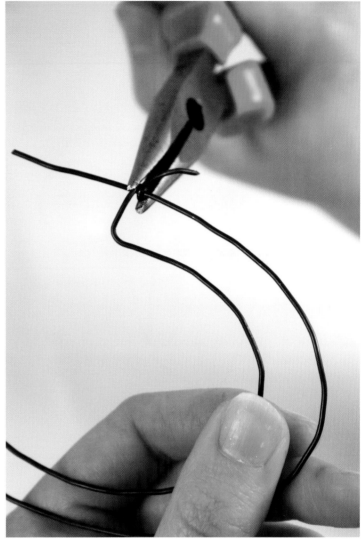

Bind the short wire around the long wire to join the handle.

To make the handle, take a length of about 50cm (19 ¾ in.) of 1.2mm (US gauge 16) iron wire and bend into the handle shape shown in the photo. Again you can use your fingers to shape and use the pliers to perfect later.

Keep measuring the handle against the teapot body and adjust so that you get the handle in proportion. There should be two loose wires towards the top of the handle; here you want to bind the shorter wire around the longer one to join the two together. Don't cut any excess wire from the longer wire, as you will need this next.

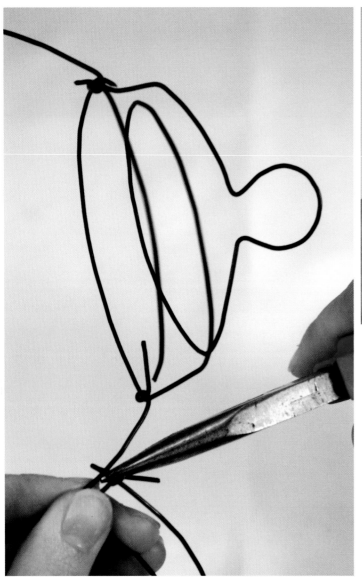

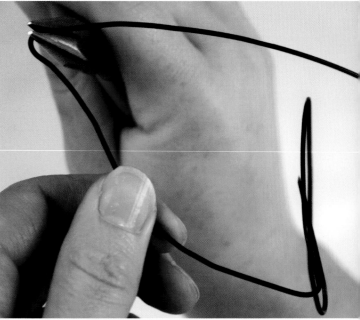

(Above) Form an oval, then bend the wire at right angles and curve to form half a spout shape.

Bind excess long wire from handle to the side of the teapot.

Place the handle at the side of the teapot and decide where you want it to go. When in position use the excess long wire to bind the handle to the edge of the teapot.

Next make the spout. Take a 40cm (15 ¾ in.) length of 1.2mm (US gauge 16) wire and form an oval to a length of about 4cm (1½in.). At the bottom of the oval bend the wire out at right angles and gently curve it and kick it back out again to form a spout shape as in the photo.

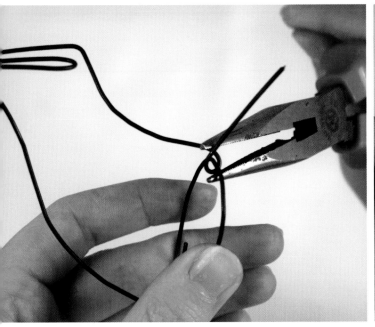

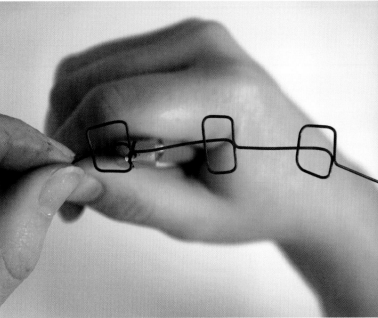

Form a small oval and then bring the wire parallel to the previous curve. Bind to the large oval and then to the side of the teapot.

Bend the wire into a square then bend left through the square. Leave a 2–3cm (approx. 1in.) gap then make your second square and continue until all the wire has been used.

Bend the wire back towards the oval and create another smaller oval, finishing so that the wire ends up facing the big oval. This is the spout hole. Bend the wire back towards the big oval so it runs parallel to the other curve. When it hits the big oval, bind the loose wire to it. Make sure to leave some excess wire, as you will need it to bind the now finished spout to the other side of the teapot. Do this just as you did with the handle.

Once the teapot structure is complete, it's time to start making the inside pattern. For this you will need about a 1.5m (58½in.) length of the thinner 0.7mm (US gauge 21) wire. Bend the wire into a square using the snipe-nose pliers. I would recommend making it about 1cm (⅜in.) but it doesn't have to be exact, it is good to vary the sizes to encourage character! When you have your first square, bend the wire to the left so it runs through the middle of the square and then start to make another square, leaving a 2–3cm (approx. 1in.) gap from the first square. Continue making squares with an equidistant gap between each until you run out of wire.

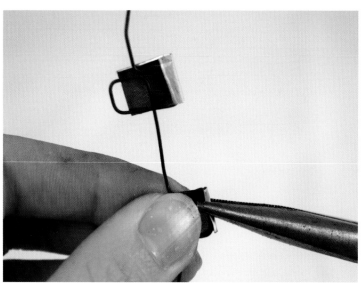

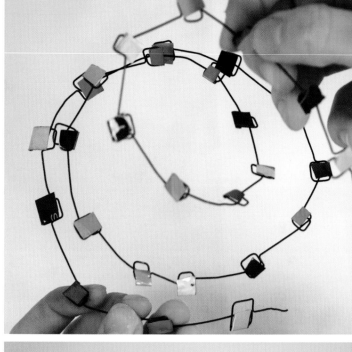

(Above) *Bend the short end of the tin around the short end of the wire.*

(Right) *Gently coil the squares on the wire with your fingers.*

(Below right) *Bind one end of the squares on the wire to the top left of the teapot. Then bind the other end to the bottom left of the teapot.*

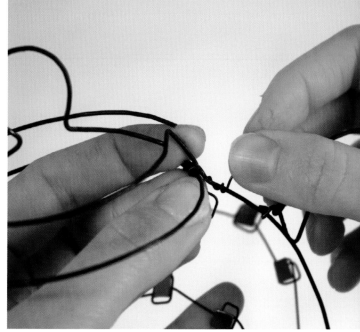

Now you need to get your tin, and using the snips (and gloves) cut out rectangles of a similar size to the wire squares, making sure you have a rectangle for each wire square. The rectangles need to be longer than the squares, as you will need to be able to tab the tin to them. I chose four complementary colours from a couple of different tins, with even numbers of each colour. Place a tin rectangle up to a wire square and using the household pliers bend one of the shorter sides of the tin around one wire square edge. Then squeeze down hard with the pliers to make sure the tin doesn't fall off. Don't worry if the tin doesn't completely cover the square as this will make it look more organic.

Do this to each wire square, alternating the colours as you go,

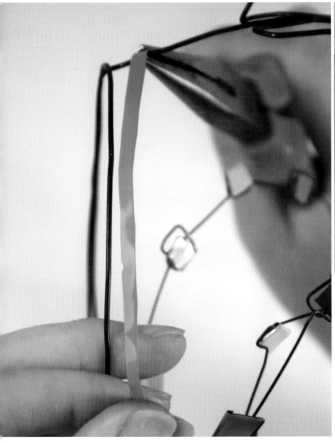

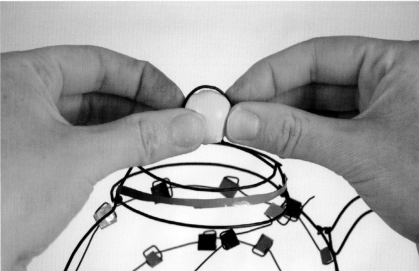

(Left) *Bend thin strips of tin around wires at the bottom of the teapot, around the lid and length of the spout. You will need to measure the strip against where you want to place it and cut off any excess tin before tabbing tin around the wires.*
(Above) *Gently push the bead into the hole created at the beginning at the top of the teapot.*

and when it is finished gently curl all the squares into a loose coil as shown in the photo.

Now get one end of the coil and bind it to the top-right corner of the teapot just below the lid. You will probably be able to do this with your fingers as you are using thinner wire. Make sure the squares sit in a nice loose coil in the middle of the teapot so that they appear to sit in space and then bind the other end to the bottom, left corner of the teapot, under the handle.

Now go back to your source of tin and cut three thin strips about 15cm (6in.) long (roughly 5mm/¼in. wide) in one of the chosen colours. You will use these strips as trimming around

the teapot bottom, along the inner line of the spout and around the lid. Bend the tin into position as you did with the squares, but this time bend the ends of the tin strips around the thicker structural wires.

Last but not least comes the bead, which will act as a decorative bobble on the teapot lid, adding extra colour and a bit of solidity. Place the bead into the wire hole you created at the beginning. Hopefully, the hole should be slightly smaller than the bead so you can push it in and the wire will hold it. However, if not, just gently squeeze the wires towards each other before inserting the bead – a bit of glue always helps too!

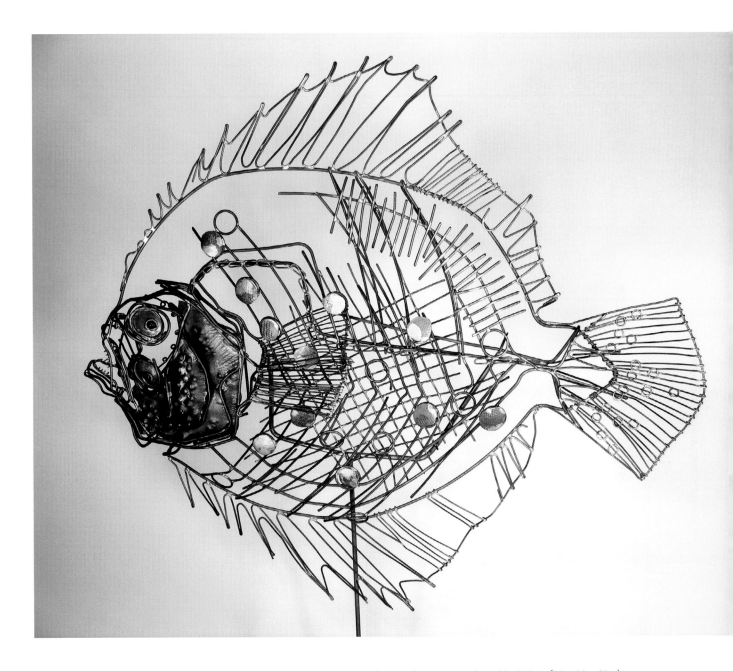

Flat Fish *by Thomas Hill, 2005. Steel wire, copper sheet, enamel paint. Dimensions: 51 x 55 x 7.5cm (20 x 22 x 3in.).* Photo courtesy of the artist.

'This piece was inspired by drawings made at the incredible Walter Rothschild Zoological Museum in Tring, Hertfordshire.' Colour has been used on this piece through the skilful use of enamel paint on copper sheet.

(Opposite) *Standing figure by Rachel Ducker, 2008. Annealed steel wire and enamelled copper for hair. Ht: 30–40cm (11 ¾–15 ¾ in.).* Photo courtesy of the artist.

CHAPTER 5

THE SHEEP

This project uses champagne-coloured copper mesh. By playing with the mesh I discovered that if you cut it into strips and scrunched it up, the edges curled. This reminded me of a coarse wiry sheep's coat and inspired me to make a complete sheep using many loose free lines to complement the messy wire mesh. I use a lot of 0.7mm (US gauge 21) iron wire in this project, which is good for giving wobbly lines and will lend the sculpture a different look. As I am now known as 'the bird lady' for my many bird sculptures, anything on four legs was a bit of a challenge!

For this project you will need some 1.2mm (US gauge 16) and 0.7mm (US gauge 21) iron wire, a small pack of coated copper mesh and two small dark beads (ideally ones that have a flat back and front rather than being completely round, a diameter of about 5mm/³⁄₁₆in. would be the best size).

MATERIALS

- Black iron wire or black annealed steel wire (1.2mm and 0.7mm/US gauge 16 and 21)
- Coloured copper mesh preferably white or cream colour
- Two small black beads, approx. 5mm/³⁄₁₆in. diameter

TOOLS

- Snipe-nose pliers
- Household pliers
- Wire cutters
- Scissors
- Araldite glue

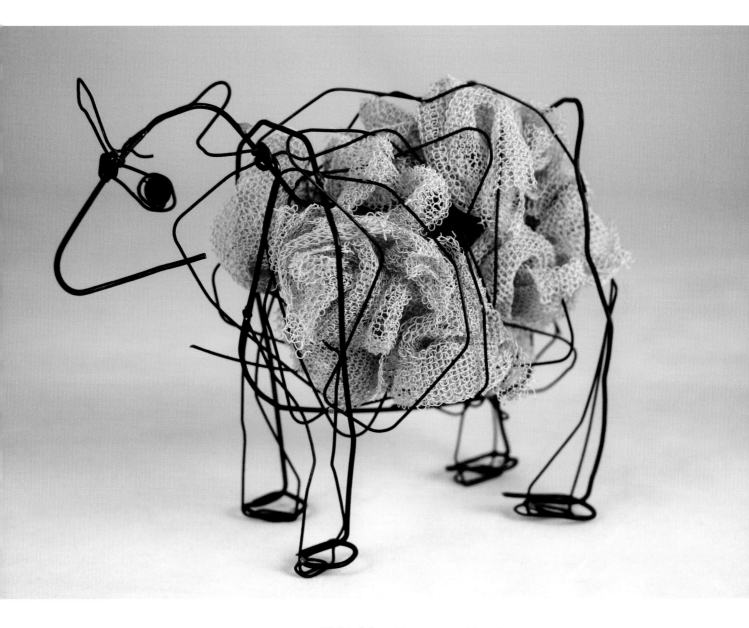

Finished sheep. Photo courtesy of the author.

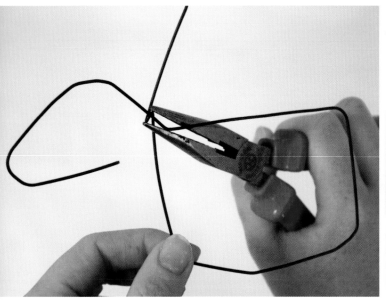

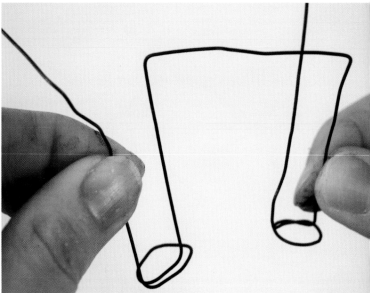

Bend the 1.2mm (US gauge 16) wire into the following shape using snipe-nose pliers. The rectangle should be around 10cm (4in.) in length. You should finish off by binding the loose wire to the neck.

Using a 60cm (23 ½ in.) strip of 0.7mm bend in the middle to form a 1cm (⁴⁄₁₀ in.) circle, then bend upwards 5cm (⅛ in.), then bend right, then at 6cm (2½in.) bend back down to form another circle making sure the two circles are the same height, then bend the wire back up to form an inner leg and bind where the wire touches the parallel line. Do not cut off any excess wire.

Start with a 40–50cm (16–20in.) strip of 1.2mm (US gauge 16) of iron wire, then using the snipe-nosed pliers bend the wire into a V and curve it round to create a lateral view of a sheep's head, as the photo demonstrates. Continue the wire by bending out horizontally, then form a rectangle with curvy edges, again following the photo, which demonstrates the shape. The rectangle should be about 10cm (4in.) long and the loose wire should finish up by the neck, where it should then be bound in position and any loose ends chopped off with wire cutters. This now constitutes a rough body and head.

Next get a 60cm (24in.) length of 0.7mm (US gauge 21) iron wire. This piece will be the beginning of the legs and hooves. Find the middle of the wire and bend at right angles, then bend the wire into a small circle approximately 1cm (⅜ in.) in diameter. Keep forming the circle round until the wire ends up parallel to the other vertical wire, then, bend upwards at right angles so it looks like you have made a three-dimensional stump. Next bend the wire to the right, about 5cm (2in.) along from the circle, at right angles. Then bend it back down at 6cm (2⅜in.) from the last bend and run the wire parallel to the other stump. Now form a circle as you did previously, making sure you do this in the right place so that the two stumps are the same length. Form the

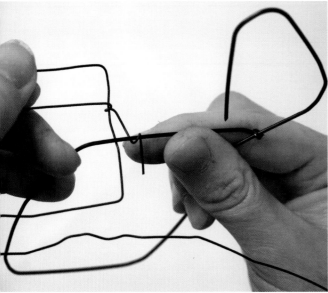

Keeping the legs together, use the excess wire from the previous bind to attach them to the front of the body. Make sure the legs are centred before tightening.

Bind the long wire from the leg to the back of the sheep. Chop off any excess wire.

circle in towards the wire structure so the loose wire, when coming up from the circle, runs upwards to form an inside leg. This wire should hit the top horizontal wire, where it should be then bound to keep it in position. Don't chop off any excess wire though, as you will need this next.

Next, bind this pair of rough legs to the front of the body. Position the legs against the vertical wire of the rectangle that forms the front of the body next to the head. Place the horizontal leg line about half way up and then bind it to the body using the excess wire from the previous binding. Make sure that the legs are centred before you bind them in place.

There should be a long straggly piece of wire dangling from one of the fore legs; bind this around the wire that makes the back of the sheep, then chop off any excess wire.

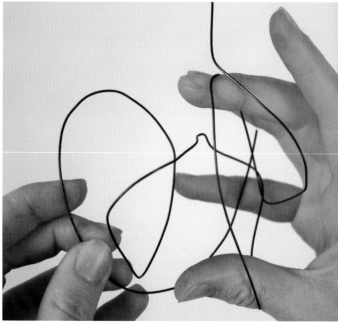

Bind the hind legs to the body as you did with the fore legs but this time bind to the rear of the rectangle. Before you tighten the bind, make sure the hind legs are in the same position as the fore legs. They need to be the same length, otherwise the sheep will not stand up.

Make a loose ball out of 0.7mm (US gauge 21) iron wire using your hands. Shape it to a similar size as the body of the sheep.

Repeat the process, this time for the hind legs. Make them exactly as you did before, but this time bind the completed legs to the back of the rectangle (where a tail would be). Make sure you position them so they are the same height as the front ones, otherwise you will have difficulty making the sheep stand. Once in the correct place, bind the long loose wire next to where you bound the other long wire from the fore legs.

Now place the sheep on its feet and see if it will stand, here you will need to gently adjust the wire with your hands so that the weight falls evenly on each foot. It does not need to stand perfectly as it will be reinforced later, but it shouldn't fall over.

Next we need to work on the structure of the body, which will hold the copper-mesh coat. For this take a good length of 0.7mm (US gauge 21) iron wire (perhaps 1m/13ft) and loosely work it into a rough ball with your fingers. The

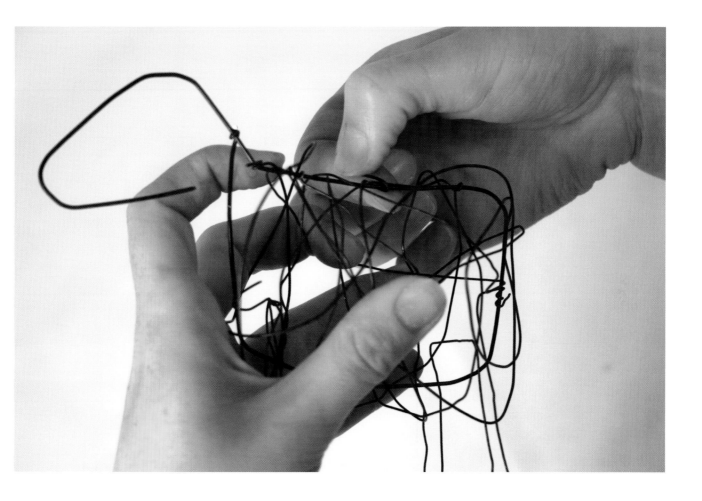

Nestle the wire ball into and around the frame of the body. When in position find the ends of the wire ball and bind these to the frame of the body to keep it in place.

ball should be about the same size as, or a little bit bigger than, the body of the sheep, and it should be quite loose so that there are plenty of gaps (you don't want the ball all screwed up and tightly packed together).

Nestle the ball around the body of the sheep, so it sits gently inside the rectangle and spills over the edges. When you have it in position, find the ends of the wire ball and gently bind the ends to the wire rectangle frame.

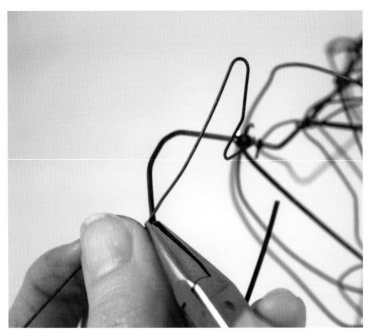 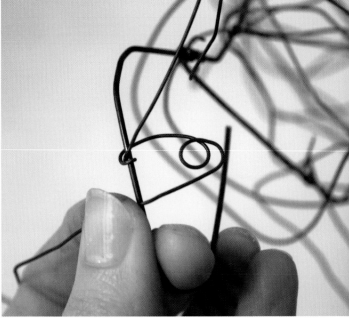

Bind a 20cm (8in.) length of 0.7mm (US gauge 21) to the back of the sheep's neck, then after a 2cm (¾in.) gap bend upwards to create an ear shape. Then bring wire towards the middle of the head and bind to the thicker wire line making sure the length of wire ends up towards the newly formed ear.

Bend the wire into a small circle the same size as your black bead, then bring the wire back towards the thicker wire and gently bend back towards the other side of the head.

The next job is to make the sheep's ears and eyes. To do this, take a 20cm (8in.) length of 0.7mm (US gauge 21) wire and bind one of the ends to the wire that makes up the sheep's neck. Position the bound wire towards the front of the head and then after about 2cm (¾ in.) bend the wire upwards into a curve, which will make up the first ear. Then bring the wire down towards the middle of the wire line that makes up the head, and bind here. Make sure you don't cut off any excess, as you want the length of wire to end up back towards the ear you just made.

Next take the length of wire and form a small circle, the approximate size of your black bead, where you think the sheep's eye should go. When you have done this, bend the wire back towards the thicker wire that makes up the head and then around to the other side.

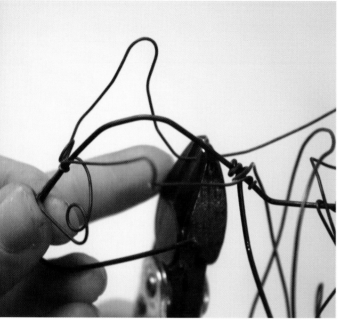

Create another circle on the other side of the head and then bend the wire upwards to form another ear shape. When formed, chop off any excess wire.

Gently encourage the strips of mesh to curl at the edges by rolling in the palm of your hands and then push the mesh balls into the gaps in the wire body until it looks full all the way around.

Now, with the wire at the other side of the head, bend it into a small circle as you did previously and then immediately bend it back upwards to form another ear shape similar to the one made on the other side. Then, instead of binding it back to the neck, just chop off any excess wire, leaving the ear free.

Next make the sheep's coat: get the colour-coated copper mesh and cut into 2–3cm (¾–1¼ in.) strips using scissors. Gently roll each strip around in your hands, encouraging the ends of the mesh to curl up, so you end up with twisted, curled ball shapes. When you have a number of them, gently push the mesh into the gaps created by the wires that make up the body. There should be enough loose wires to contain the mesh; it should feel a bit like stuffing a toy. When you are finished stuffing, the body should appear full and the mesh should add some good all-round texture.

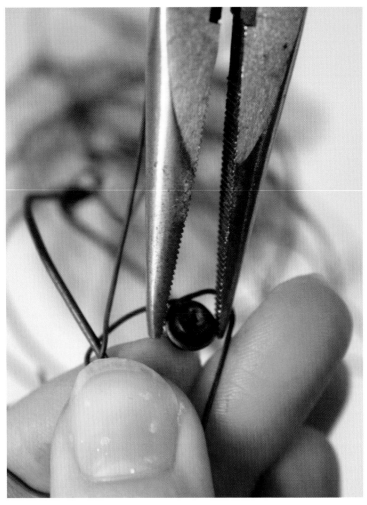

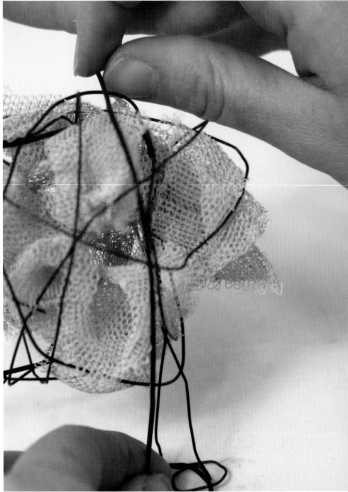

(Above left) *Place the black beads in the small circles that make up the eyes and then squeeze with household pliers to keep in position.*

(Above right) *Place support over the body, getting the circles as close as possible to the original legs so they are touching.*

(Right) *Mix up some Araldite and place a couple of spots where the two wires touch each other by the feet.*

Carefully go around the body with Araldite placing spots of glue where the wires and mesh happen to touch each other.

Next take the two black beads and place each one in the small circles that make up the eyes. When in position, gently squeeze with the household pliers to keep in position.

The sheep is now nearly complete, but to make it more stable we need to add some thicker wire to the legs. To do this cut two 40cm (16in.) lengths of 1.2mm (US gauge 16) wire. Take one of the wires and form a 1cm (⅜in.) circle at one end, then bend the length of wire at right angles so it is pointing upwards. Place this against the hind legs so the circle is next to the sheep's foot, then bend the wire around the top of the body and back down towards the other hind leg. When the wire touches the ground, form another 1cm (⅜in.) circle, then trim any excess wire. Do the same with the other wire, but this time around the fore legs. Get each support and place in its position over the body at the front and the back, getting the circles as close to the original legs as possible so they are touching.

Mix up some Araldite and place a couple of spots of the glue where the thick and thin wires touch each other.

Finally, to make sure everything holds together carefully go around the body of the sheep with Araldite, placing spots of glue where the wires happen to touch each other and the mesh. This will make sure it does not collapse.

Now you have a complete sheep, you could make smaller versions to create lambs … then all you need are a farmer, a field and a sheepdog!

The Wire Boys *by Helen Godfrey, 2007. Aviary wire. Life-size.*
'I tend to use aviary wire. I love the human form, but as I live in the Dorset countryside I am very inspired by wildlife around me.' Photos by artist.

The Gardener *by Helen Godfrey, 2007. Made from aviary wire. Life-size.*
'I prefer to leave the wire that lovely grey colour rather than spray it, as I like to think of it as a 3D pencil drawing.'

(Opposite) **Young Guinea Fowl Running** *by Celia Smith, 2007. Steel wire, brass wires and telephone cabling. Ht: 32cm (12 ½in.).*

Photo by Peter Stone.

'I wanted to build up a dense plumage for this guinea fowl so I layered lots of thin brass wires over a steel wire frame. I then sewed on washers to give an indication of its spots.'

(Above) **Peacock Feathered Hat** *by Alison Bailey Smith, 2006. Wearable wire hat made from lacquered copper reclaimed from old televisions. Intricately knotted and looped to create a lacey 'fabric' and structure simultaneously. Lined for comfort and designed to be worn.*

Photo by Richard Jennings of Cetra, Heswall. Model: Anh.

CHAPTER 6

THE BI-PLANE

This project demonstrates some of the more advanced skills used in creating wire sculpture. So far we have relied on binding two wires together to create a join. Here, however, the use of silver solder will be introduced, to provide a much smoother join. It is worth bearing in mind that there are health and safety issues when soldering, as you are dealing with high heat, and the process does require a few more tools than you would get from your standard DIY shop.

We will be making a bi-plane out of copper wire, some rubber washers, coloured card and spray paint. I love the way bi-planes appear to have their own personality with their variety of colours and markings. You can personalise yours too, with your own logos and colour choices.

We are using copper in this project, rather than iron wire, as it is a good material to solder with. Copper has a very different quality to iron: it is very soft and malleable and becomes even softer when you heat it up during the soldering process. This will take a bit of getting used to after using the iron, as you will have to be careful not to distort the shapes you create!

MATERIALS
- Copper wire (1.2 and 0.9mm/US gauge 16 and 19)
- Flat-nose pliers
- Snipe-nose pliers
- Spray paint
- 2 washers approximately 2.5cm (1in.) in diameter
- 2 washers approximately 1.5cm (½ in.) in diameter
- Coloured card (red, white and blue, but you can use other colours)

HEALTH & SAFETY
- Always wear goggles when soldering
- Beware hot wires – allow to cool before touching
- Don't leave gas torch on unlit

TOOLS
- Flat-nose pliers
- Snipe-nose pliers
- Wire cutters
- Scissors
- Household pliers
- Borax cone and dish
- Easy solder
- Large soldering block
- Reverse action tweezers with insulated handle
- Small natural bristle paintbrush
- Stainless steel tweezers
- Safety goggles
- Handheld gas torch
- Old toothbrush or bottlebrush

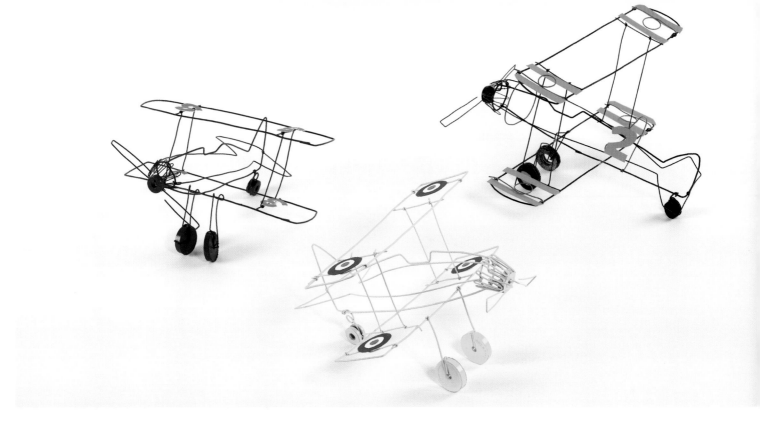

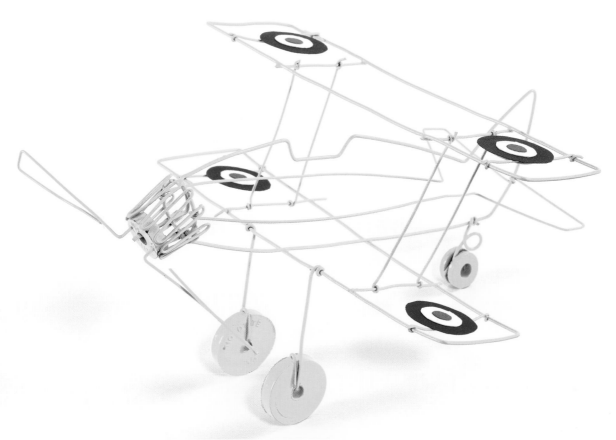

Colourful bi-planes from the Bi-plane Project, by Cathy Miles. Dimensions: approx. 25 x 22cm (10 x 8 ¾in.). Photo by Simon Winnall.

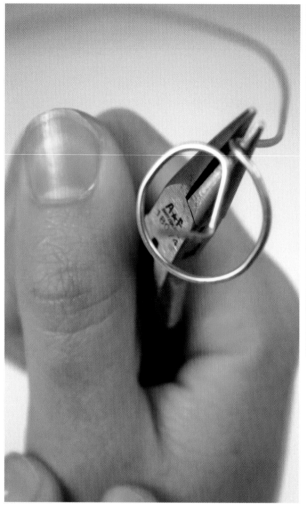

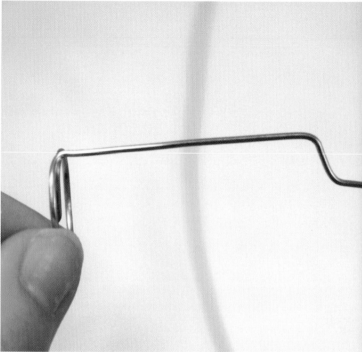

(Left) At 2cm (¾in.) from the end bend the wire at right angles, then immediately form a 2cm (¾in.) diameter circle around this point. When complete, bend the wire at right angles from the circle so it runs away from the other end of the wire.
(Above) About 5cm (2in.) along from the circle make a trough shape for the imaginary pilot.

Start by cutting a 1m (3ft) length of 1.2mm (US gauge 16) copper wire and running a scouring pad down the length of it to remove any dirt or grease. I would prepare all the copper wire needed for this project before doing anything else, as it is important to keep your surfaces clean when soldering.

This wire will form the basic body shape, so: 2cm (¾in.) from one end bend the wire with a pair of snipe-nose pliers at right angles then immediately form a circle around this bend about 2cm (¾in.) in diameter. Then bend the wire so it runs at right angles to the circle, pointing away from the other end of wire.

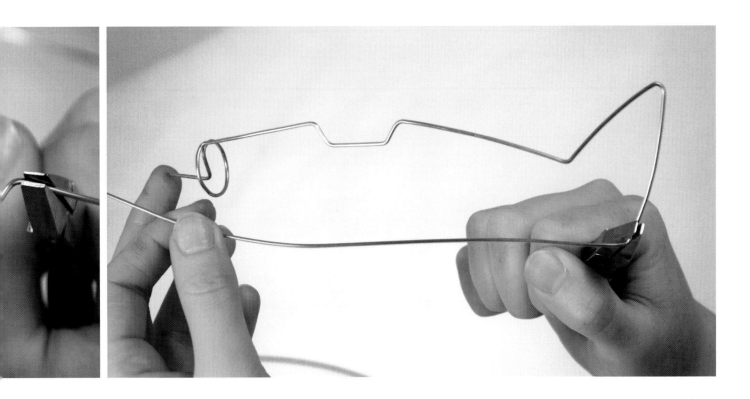

Bend the wire upwards into a point to create a tail. Then, bend the wire back down again and across towards the circle where you should securely bind it.

This wire is going to make up the top side of the aeroplane body, so make a trough shape about 2cm (¾ in.) long by 1cm (⅜ in.) deep with your pliers about 5cm (2in.) along; this is the cockpit where your imaginary pilot will sit.

Now continue this wire line for another 5cm (2in.), then bend the wire upwards into a point and bring it back down again to form the aeroplane tail, making it about 4cm (1½ in.) tall. When you have made the tail bend the wire back towards your original circle and bind to it securely, cutting off any excess.

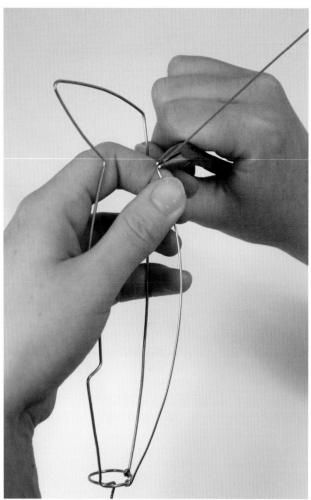

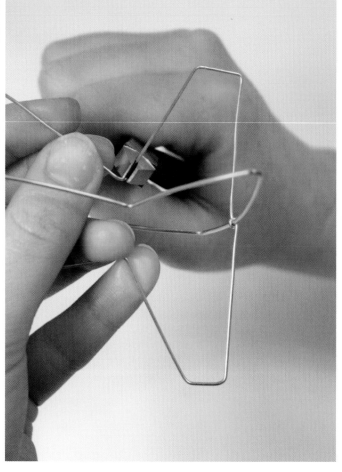

Attach the 0.9mm (US gauge 19) wire to the circle and run the wire to the point where the tail starts. Here bend out at a slight angle.

Bend the side tail into the shape demonstrated in the photo, then bind it to the thicker original tail before repeating the same tail shape on the other side.

Next we need to create the sides of the aeroplane body. To do this, cut a metre length of thinner 0.9mm (US gauge 19) copper wire. Bind one end to the circle then run the wire down to the point where the tail begins.

At this point bend the wire out at a slight angle (as the photo demonstrates) to create a side tail. Bend the wire towards the thicker tail wire and bind them where the two touch to keep them in place. Repeat the tail shape along the other side and bring the wire back up to the front so you can bind it to the circle to keep it in position.

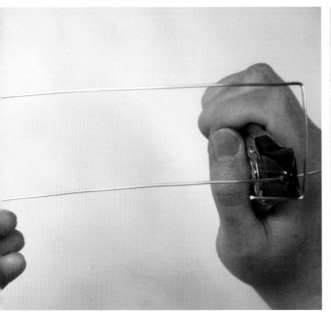

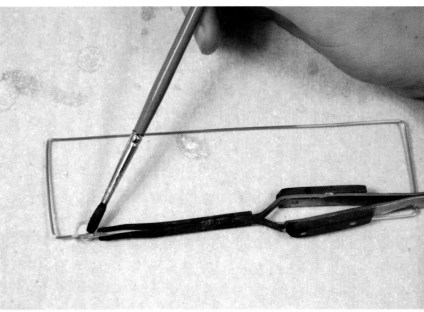

Bend 1.2mm (US gauge 16) copper wire into two rectangles approximately 30 x 5cm (12 x 2in.) each. Make sure there is about a 1cm (⅜in.) overlap of copper wire.

Use reverse-action tweezers to hold the overlap together so the wires touch. Apply borax and a pallion of solder using a paintbrush or tweezers.

Now that you have a body shape, you need to make some wings. For this take a decent length of 1.2mm (US gauge 16) copper wire and form two rectangles about 30 x 5cm (11¾ x 2in.). You may find it easier to use flat nose pliers for this, as they will help you to achieve straighter lines. Before cutting off the excess wire, make sure there is an overlap of wire (about 1cm/⅜in.) as this is where your solder join will go.

Place a wire rectangle on your soldering block and use a pair of reverse-action tweezers to gently hold the overlapping wires together. This may be a little tricky; you might need to practise getting the tweezers in the right spot. Make sure that the two wires are actually touching.

Now make up a borax paste with your borax cone and dish and cut some pallions of easy solder with your tin snips, placing them in the borax dish. Apply the borax paste to your soldering join with the paintbrush and then pick up a pallion of solder either with your damp paintbrush, as I do, or with a pair of stainless-steel tweezers.

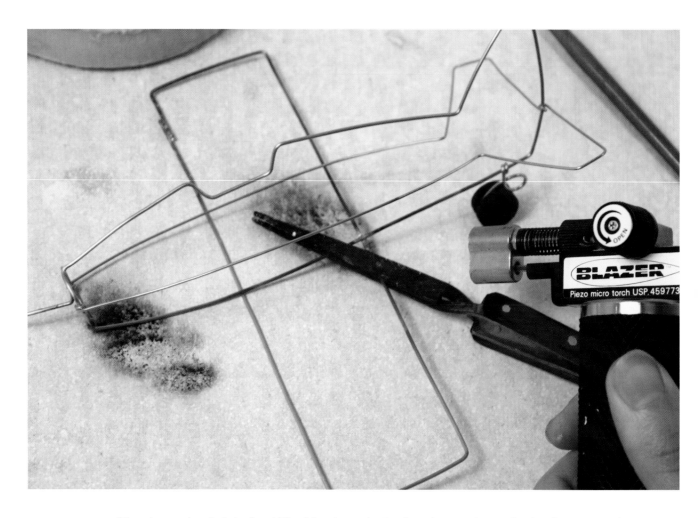

Place the aeroplane body in the middle of the wing and grip where the two wires touch using the reverse-action tweezers.
Then solder in both places.

Now put your goggles on and get your gas torch, placing it on the soldering block. Put the torch on so you have a large flame and then adjust the dial that controls the air pressure to form a good soft blue flame. Keep the torch in one hand and the steel tweezers in the other. Take the torch to your rectangle and gently heat the area of the solder join. The borax will start to bubble, if the solder moves off the join, be ready with your tweezers to place back in the correct area. When soldering you need to apply heat evenly, so make sure you keep moving the flame from one side to the other so both sides of the join are equally hot. When the area is hot, concentrate the flame

directly on the solder joint, gently moving from left to right along the wire. Get the wires red-hot so that the solder will melt and then run along the overlap. When this happens you can turn off the torch and allow the rectangle to cool before taking it off the block. If the solder doesn't run, ask yourself the following questions: Is the join clean? Did you de-grease the copper? Are the wires actually touching each other? Is it hot enough, did you apply enough heat? Has the solder pallion fallen off? Does borax cover the complete joint? Have you used enough solder?

When you have successfully soldered your joint, do the

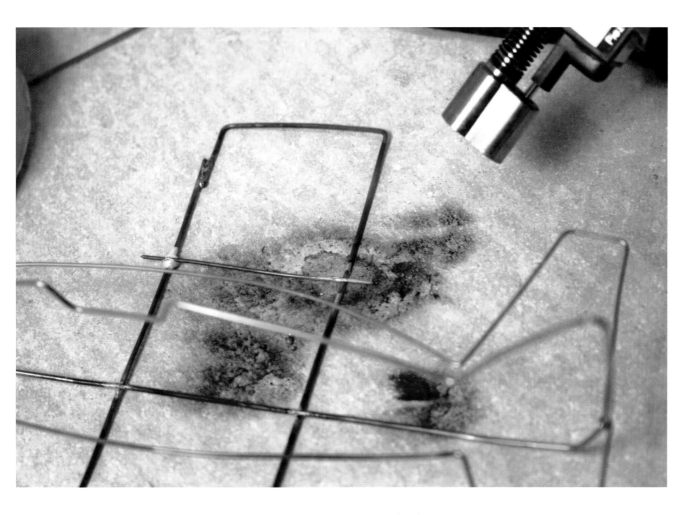

Place a length of wire 5cm (2in.) in from the end of each wing tip. Then solder in place.

same with the second rectangle and leave to cool. Next, take the aeroplane body and position it on the top of a wing section in the centre. Make sure the cockpit is facing upwards, then secure in place with the reverse-action tweezers, capturing both the wing and body as shown in the photo. The wing should touch the body in two places; both need to be soldered to keep it in position. Start with one join, using the borax and soldering just as you did previously. Then, when cool, move the tweezers round to secure the second join before soldering.

You may find that some of the lines become slightly distorted during the soldering process because the heat makes the copper softer. You may need to straighten out these wobbles. I would recommend using the flat-nose pliers for this.

Next cut four 6cm (2½ in.) lengths of 0.9mm (US gauge 19) copper wire. Get two lengths and place along the width of the wing (soldered to the body) about 5cm (2in.) from each end. Then solder where the wires meet and trim off any excess copper protruding from the edges. This time you shouldn't need the reverse-action tweezers as the wires will naturally sit flush to each other. Do the same for the second wing that has not yet been attached.

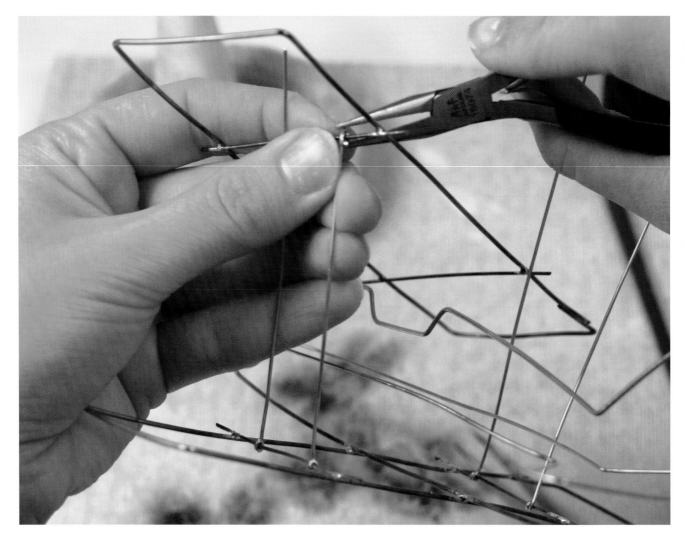

With your four vertical wires in place on the lower wing, place the upper wing about 6cm (2⅜in.) directly above, then bind into position on the cross bars.

These crossbars will act as a place to attach some vertical wires, which in turn will hold the wings parallel to each other. So to do this, cut eight 10cm (4in.) lengths of 0.9mm (US gauge 19) copper wire and carefully bind two lengths to each crossbar, approximately 2cm (¾in.) apart. Make sure that the binds are tight; I would secure them with the smaller snipe-nose pliers as the heavy-duty ones with grips running along the inside will mark the soft copper wire. When you have the four vertical wires in place on the lower wing, take your upper wing and place it directly above,

aiming for an approximate 6cm (2⅜in.) gap between the two. When in the right place, bind in position to the crossbars. You may want to solder over the binds to get a really solid structure; this won't be too difficult as the wires are already held in place, so you won't have to use unwieldy tweezers.

Now the wings are in position, it is time to work on the nose of the plane. To do this, take 50cm (20in.) of copper 0.9mm (US gauge 19) wire and your flat-nosed pliers. With the pliers bend this wire up and down to form a zigzag pattern;

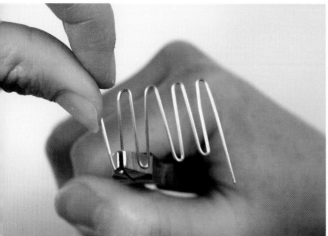

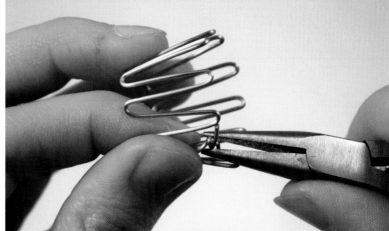

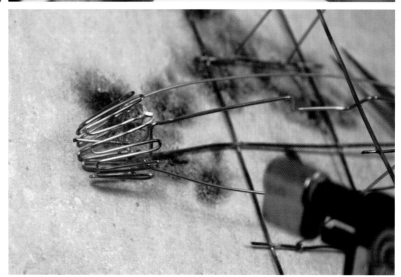

(Above left) *With the 0.9mm (US gauge 19) copper wire form a zigzag pattern approximately 2cm (¾in.) high using the flat-nose pliers.*

(Above right) *Bind the excess wire to one of the zigzags to keep it in place.*

(Right) *Place the zigzags over the circle at the nose and solder in a position where the zigzags and circle touch each other.*

I think that flat-nose pliers help to get sharper bends, which are good for the zigzags. Make them about 2cm (¾in.) high and continue until you have about a 6cm (2⅜in.) length of pattern.

Now curl your length of zigzag into a circle and position it against the nose of the plane. You want the zigzags to fit over the circle of the nose, so see how big the circle needs to be and then trim accordingly, leaving a very small amount of excess wire. Use this excess wire to bind to one of the zigzags to keep it in place, and complete the circle, as demonstrated in the photo.

Now we need to attach the zigzags to the circle on the nose of the plane. To do this, push the zigzags over the circle, so they sit on it and the two just overlap. Hopefully it should stay in place, because there should be some tension in the zigzags as they gently stretch over the circle. However, if it doesn't easily stay in position just use the tweezers to keep it in place. There should be a couple of places where the circle and zigzags touch. Choose one place and then solder to keep the two together. One solder join should be enough.

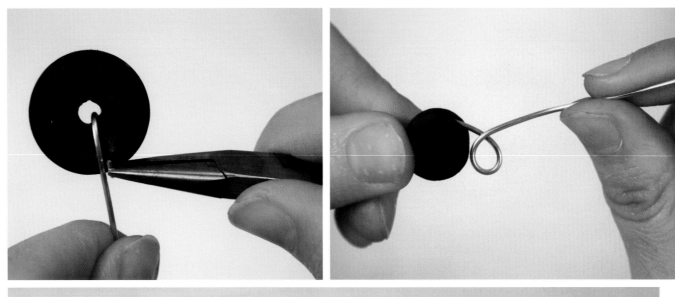

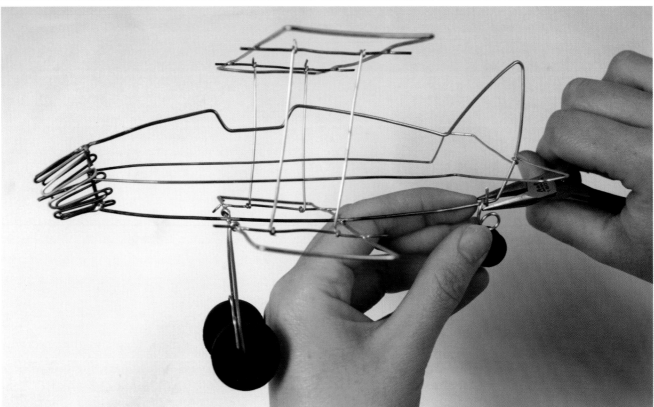

(Top left) *Put a length of 1.2mm (US gauge 16) copper wire through the hole of the washer and bind round to the other side, tightening with pliers to keep it in position.*

(Top right) *Secure the copper wire to the small washer, then form a small circle immediately next to it.*
(Above) *Bind the smaller wheel to the rear of the aeroplane and bind the two larger front wheels to the lower wing.*

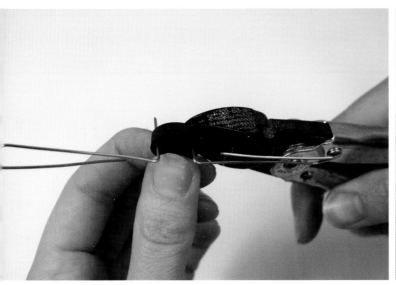

Create a wire wedge shape out of 0.9mm (US gauge 19) wire, cutting one end short and bending the other at right angles. Then push the wire through the small rubber washer until it goes right through to the other side. Place both wedges so they face opposite each other and then trim any excess wire from the back of the washer.

Gently squeeze the zigzags against the washer to gain a tighter fit.

This is the last solder join of the project, so the next job will be to remove all the excess borax from the copper. For this, I would recommend placing the aeroplane in a tub of hot water with some Fairy Liquid. Allow to soak for a few minutes, then get a bottlebrush or toothbrush to gently scrub the solder joins. This should help to get rid of any excess, but don't do it too aggressively as you may misshape the wire.

Next make the front wheels. To do this, take the two large washers and cut two lengths of copper wire to 1.2mm (US gauge 16) each. Put the length of the wire through the hole in the washer, bind it round through to the other side, then squeeze with pliers to tighten into position. Then repeat with the other washer.

Next do the same with a small washer. When the copper wire has been secured, form a small circle as shown in the photo. When you have done this, cut the wire so you only have about 2cm (¾in.) excess, then bind it to the bottom rear of the aeroplane with the circle facing towards the tail.

Next take the front wheels and cut the copper wire so you have a 6cm (2⅜in.) length. Then take one wheel and bind it to the bottom wing, along the long edge that is nearest the nose. Bind it 2cm (¾in.) from the middle of the wing to the left. Then get the other front wheel and bind it 2cm (¾in.) from the middle to the right. Try to make sure that you bind it in the right place so the two wheels are the same height, as you don't want a wobbly aeroplane!

Now the aeroplane should stand on its wheels as if getting ready for take-off. But it's still missing the front propeller. For this get a length of 0.9mm (US gauge 19) wire and bend into a wedge shape as shown in the photo. Make it about 5cm (2in.) long, then, bend one length at right angles. Trim the other side so it sits short of the right angle. Repeat this so you have a pair. Now get a small washer and using pliers poke the two wedges through the rubber washer. This is easy enough to do because rubber is soft and also likes to naturally grip things, so once the wedges are in they won't fall out. Make

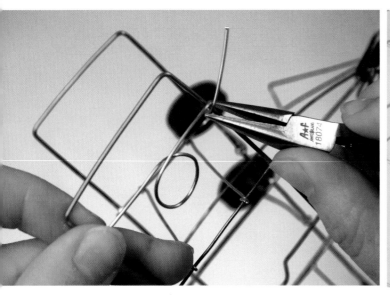

Bind a circle in the corner of each wing.

Place Araldite along the wire circles and then place the card circles in position on top.

sure you position them so they face in opposite directions, like propellers, and then cut off any excess wire.

Now take the washer and place it on your aeroplane nose so the propellers face outwards; it should sit gently under the zigzags. To keep it in place you can gently squeeze the zigzags to the washer for a tighter fit; if this fails you can fix it with a spot of Araldite. Finally, it's time for the decoration – time to personalise your plane and give it some character. You can do this in a variety of ways with different paints, papers and fabrics, but for this plane I will be making some simple coloured roundels to put on the wings. To glue card onto the aeroplane you will need a frame: make four circles out of 0.9mm (US gauge 19) wire about 1cm (⅜in.) in diameter, attach one to each wing corner by binding to the two long sides, then trim any excess wire.

Now we need to spray the plane, so get some old newspaper to protect your work surfaces and place the plane on the newspaper in a well-ventilated area. I decided to paint my plane yellow and I used a fast-dry enamel paint that gives a lovely glossy

surface, though any spray paint will do. It is best to build up the paint in a few thin layers then one thick layer. Make sure the paint is dry before applying the next layer, otherwise you end up with a bit of a gooey mess!

While you are waiting for the paint to dry, get your three colours of card. Cut out four big circles in one colour (about 2.5cm/1in. in diameter), four medium circles in another colour (about 2cm/¾in. in diameter) and finally four small circles in the other colour (about 1.5cm/⅝in. in diameter). When you have these, use some Pritt stick and glue a medium circle on top of a big circle and a small circle to the medium circle so you end up with four card circles.

When your aeroplane is dry and evenly coated, mix up some Araldite and apply to the wire circle detail on the wings. Then place a card circle on each wire circle and allow to dry.

Now you have a finished bi-plane! You could add fancy graphics to the detail or perhaps pop a photo of your grandad in the pilot's seat!

GALLERY

Leaping Unicorn *by Ed Netley, 2007. Made using 3.15mm (Us gauge 8) galvanised steel wire for the body and construction, with 2.5mm (US gauge 10) steel wire for finer areas. The wire is fencing wire (from a farm suppliers).* Photo by Alison Stace, courtesy of The Mythic Garden, Stone Lane Gardens.

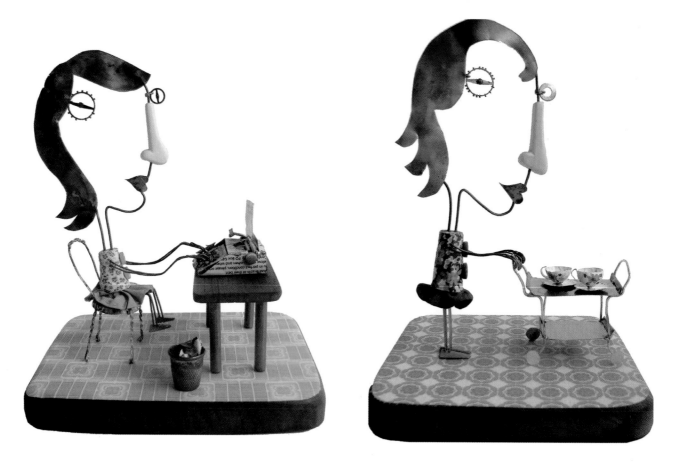

(Above) **At the Office** *and* Tea for Two *by Lauren van Helmond, 2008. Tinned wire, wood, paper, fabric, copper, recycled brass tins, clock parts and buttons. Made using hand-formed components with lead and silver soldering.* Photos by Lauren van Helmond.

(Above left) **Homage to Calder** *by Julie Griffiths Jones, 2003. Painted mild steel, aluminium, thread. Dimensions: 130 x 74cm (51 x 29in.).*
'In September 2003 I went to the Guggenheim Museum in Bilbao to see Calder's mobiles. I sat for a long time on a bench looking at a mobile
hanging on its own in an alcove whose walls were curved and undulating. I had made the paper design for this piece and tried to imagine it
hanging in this space. It is intended as a self-portrait and the underneath layer is a red 'betgwn', green bodice, lace collar and cream shawl.
These are elements of the Welsh costume, but the half-apron, although worn in Wales, is highly decorated with images from eastern
European embroidery.' Photo by Jason Ingram.
(Above right) **My Private Register** *by Blanka Sperkova, 1994. Knitted steel wire.* Photo by Jakub Dvorsky.

(Opposite, below) **Elephant Holding a Ball** *by Jim Unsworth, 1999. Made from 6mm (¼in.) and 10mm (⅜in.) steel round bar.* Photo by
Eddie Powell, courtesy of Pride of the Valley Sculpture Park.

(Above) **Subaru** *by Benedict Radcliffe, 2005. A wire frame technique was used to draw the Subaru Impreza P1, life-size in scale, in three dimensions and sprayed arctic white. It is made from 10mm (½in.) steel round bar. All welds have been filed away, giving an impression of fluidity and continuousness.* Photo courtesy of the artist.

(Opposite, top left) **Cutlery Pot** *by Cathy Miles, 2006. Iron wire and mixed materials. Dimensions: 19 x 12cm (7 ½ x 4¾in.).* Photo by Simon Winnall.

(Right) **Fatball** *by Cathy Miles, 2006. Iron wire and mixed materials. Dimensions: 28 x 37cm (11 x 14½in.).* Photo by Simon Winnall.

(Below left) *Detail of* Brain's Fairy Winch (mark 2) *by Samantha Bryan, 2004. 'New Improved Dual-Pedal-Power ensures optimum approach speed is achieved and guarantees sufficient lift for safe, successful launch. Flight Safety Legislation forced its Single-Powered predecessor to be withdrawn from service, after a spate of accidents dubbed it the "Bottom Breaker".' Brass wire & sheet, leather, paper clay & collected items. Dimensions: 70x 20 x 35cm (27½ x 8 x 13¾ in.).* Photo by Robert Leach.

'The brass structure is silver soldered together and chemically treated to give the illusion of age. The figures are created in hand-stitched leather over a wire skeleton. I am very inspired by Victorian and Edwardian invention and gadgetry. The idea for this particular piece was taken from a glider having to be winched into the air. I borrowed this concept for my fairy figures and their plight to learn to fly.'

(Right) **The Allerton Traveller** *by Samantha Bryan, 2007. Brass wire and sheet, leather, muslin, tissue paper, paper clay and found objects. Dimensions: 80 x 30 x 60cm (31½ x 12 x 23¾ in.).* Photo by Robert Leach.

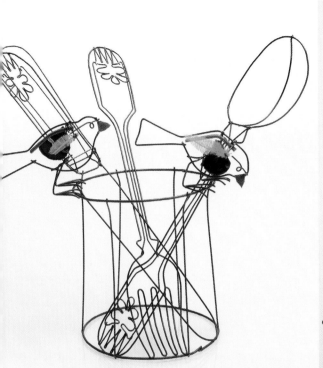

(Top) *Detail of* **Seated Figure** *by Rachel Ducker, 2006. Annealed steel wire. Life-size.* Photo courtesy of the artist.

(Above) **Baby Garden Birds** *by Cathy Miles, 2006. Iron wire and mixed materials. Dimensions: 8 x 5cm (3 x 2in.).* Photo by Simon Winnall.

(Opposite) **Seated Figure** *by Rachel Ducker, 2008. Life-size figure from annealed steel wire (some galvanised, some black).*

Photo courtesy of the artist.

APPENDICES

Below is a list of suppliers to try on your hunt for materials and tools. I have tried to choose those that have a mail order facility or are available online.

It is also worth looking in the Yellow Pages under metal merchants to see who could supply you with base metals in your area. Make sure to visit your local DIY shop to see if they stock wire, it will also be good place to get your staple wire cutters, household pliers, goggles, gloves and Araldite. Local hobby shops are also worth a visit as they can sell a good range of pliers. They may also inspire you to integrate other materials into your wire sculptures as you may find things you would never have thought to use before. Do visit car boot sales if you get the opportunity, as you can also find useful tools and unusual materials at them.

LIST OF SUPPLIERS
UK

WIRE SUPPLIERS

Scientific Wire Company
18 Raven Road, South
Woodford
London
E18 1HW
Tel: 020 8505 0002
Fax: 020 8559 1114
www.wires.co.uk
The Scientific Wire Company supplies a large variety of wires and mesh, such as iron, copper, brass and a broad range of coloured wires. They have a mail order catalogue, which is also available to view online. You can buy reasonably small quantities through them.

Edwards Metals Ltd
37A Birch Road East
Witton, Birmingham
West Midlands
B6 7DA
Tel: 0121 3222366
Fax: 0121 3269369
Edwards are good suppliers of heavy-gauge iron wire. They also sell copper, brass and gilding metal.

JEWELLERY TOOL SUPPLIERS

Cookson Precious Metals
59–83 Vittoria Street
Birmingham
B1 3NZ
Tel: 0845 100 1122/0121 200 2120
www.cooksongold.com
Cookson's is a good place to get pliers, handheld gas torches and other essential soldering equipment. They also sell thin gauge iron wire. You can order online through the website.

H.S Walsh & Sons
Head Office
243 Beckenham Rd
Beckenham
Kent
BR3 4TS
Tel: 020 8778 7061

Hatton Garden Showrooms
44 Hatton Garden
London
EC1N 8ER
Tel: 020 7242 3711

Birmingham Showrooms
1–2 Warstone Mews
Warstone Lane
Hockley
Birmingham
B18 6JB
Tel: 0121 236 9346
www.hswalsh.com
A good place to get soldering equipment, pliers and cutters. They have showrooms in London and Birmingham, but you can also purchase online or through mail order catalogue.

Thomas Sutton Limited
83 Vittoria Street
Birmingham
B1 3NZ
Tel: 0845 0941884
A good place to get soldering equipment, pliers and cutters. Their showroom is in Birmingham, which is worth a visit as they are very helpful. You can also purchase online.

TOOL SUPPLIERS

Axminster Power Tool Centre
Tel: *0800 371822*
www.axminster.co.uk
This is a massive DIY shop in a catalogue. They sell goggles, gloves, wire cutters and pliers. They offer mail order sales and have an online shop. There is also a useful technical helpline if you have questions.

OTHER USEFUL SUPPLIERS

Hobbycraft
www.hobbycraft.co.uk
Hobbycraft is a huge superstore that stocks all sorts of craft materials. It is a good place to get coloured card, fake flowers, beads, fabrics and spray paints. They do not have an online shop, but if you go to the website it will show you where your nearest outlet is.

Sportfish
Winforton
Nr Hereford
HR3 6SP
Tel: 01544 327111
www.sportfish.co.uk
Sportfish is a good place to buy fishing flies that are used in the butterfly project. They have a shop you can visit, an online store plus a mail order catalogue.

London Graphics Centre
16–18 Shelton Street
Covent Garden
London
WC2H 9JL
Tel: 020 7759 4500
www.londongraphics.co.uk
London Graphic Centre is a good place to get a broad spectrum of spray paint. It is also a good place for card and other graphic embellishments. You can visit their shop or purchase online.

Worcestershire Resource Exchange
Unit 9a
Shrub Hill Industrial Estate
Worcester
WR4 9EL
Tel: 01905 726796
www.wre.uk.com
The Worcester Resource Exchange is an organisation you can join for an annual fee. Once you are a member you are entitled to go and purchase scrap by the trolley or basket load. They have a huge variety of scrap material most of which has come from local businesses. Keep a look out for an equivalent organisation in your area.

USA

Metalliferous
34 West 46th Street
New York
NY 10036
Tel: (212) 944 0909
www.metalliferous.com
A good place for wire and pliers. You can purchase on-line or go to the store.

Paramount Wire Co.
2–8 Central Ave
East Orange
NJ 07018
Tel: (973) 672 0500
www.parawire.com
Paramount wire supplies a broad range of wires, especially black annealed wire.

WEBSITES OF ARTISTS

Alison Bailey Smith
www.abscraft.com

Samantha Bryan
www.brainsfairies.co.uk

Rachel Ducker
www.rachelducker.co.uk

Julia Griffiths Jones
www.juliagriffithsjones.co.uk

Thomas Hill
www.home.earthlink.net/~wiretom

Priscilla Jones
www.priscillajones.org.uk

Cathy Miles
www.cathymiles.com

Ed Netley
www.netzfineart.com

Benedict Radcliffe
www.benedictradcliffe.co.uk

Celia Smith
www.celia-smith.co.uk

Blanka Sperkova
www.amanitadesign.com/blankas
perkova

Jim Unsworth
www.jimunsworth.co.uk

Lauren Van Helmond
www.laurenvanhelmond.co.uk

US WIRE GAUGE SIZES

US gauge no.	Diameter in inches	Diameter in mm	US gauge no.	Diameter in inches	Diameter in mm	US gauge no.	Diameter in inches	Diameter in mm
NO. 8	0.1285	3.264	NO. 16	0.05082	1.291	NO. 24	0.02010	0.5105
NO. 9	0.1144	2.906	NO. 17	0.04526	1.150	NO. 25	0.01790	0.4547
NO. 10	0.1019	2.588	NO. 18	0.04030	1.024	NO. 26	0.01594	0.4049
NO. 11	0.09074	2.305	NO. 19	0.03589	0.9116	NO. 27	0.01420	0.3607
NO. 12	0.08081	2.053	NO. 20	0.03196	0.8118	NO. 28	0.01264	0.3211
NO. 13	0.07196	1.828	NO. 21	0.02846	0.7229	NO. 29	0.01120	0.2845
NO. 14	0.06408	1.628	NO. 22	0.02535	0.6439	NO. 30	0.01003	0.2548
NO. 15	0.05707	1.450	NO. 23	0.02257	0.5733			

INDEX